I0754763

UITGAVEN VAN HET
NEDERLANDS HISTORISCH-ARCHAEOLOGISCH INSTITUUT TE ISTANBUL

Publications de l'Institut historique et archéologique néerlandais de Stamboul

sous la direction de
E. van Donzel, A.A. Kampman,
Machteld J. Mellink et Pauline H.E. Voûte

XXXIX

MĪKHĀ'ĪL NU'AYMAH

Promoter of the Arabic Literary Revival

Mīkhā'īl Nu'aymah as octogenarian

MĪKHĀ'ĪL NU'AYMAH

Promoter of the Arabic Literary Revival

by

C. NIJLAND

NEDERLANDS HISTORISCH-ARCHAEOLOGISCH INSTITUUT
TE ISTANBUL
1975

Printed in Belgium

MĪKHĀ'ĪL NU'AYMAH

Promoter of the Arabic Literary Revival

CONTENTS

I. INTRODUCTION

Modern Arabic literature can be defined as including everything written with a self-conscious awareness of style and manner and which, in one way or the other, has contributed to the so-called *Nahḍah* (Revival) [1], the self-assertion of the Arabs against their Turkish overlords and against the western world powers which had made themselves felt in the Middle and Near East from Bonaparte's occupation of Egypt in 1797 onwards. Since this definition tends to exclude the literary products which belong to what may be considered post-*Nahḍah* literature, it is perhaps better to use a negative formulation by setting modern Arabic literature apart from the products which are considered to belong to the so-called *'aṣr al-inḥiṭāṭ* (The Age of Decline) as the revival-conscious Arabs named the period preceding their *Nahḍah*. There is a long period of transition during which poems in the traditional style were being composed and estimated. Although these poems are still being written, they have lost much of their significance on the literary scene.

The break with the preceding period manifested itself in various ways. Some poets imitated the poems of the so-called Golden Period [2]; others followed western models; and still others, probably under the impression of romantic literary theories, advocated the originality of the creative artist. Both region and religion exerted their influence on the various currents which can be discerned in modern Arabic literature.

The bases of the *Nahḍah* go back as far as the French occupation of Egypt (1797-1801) and the reign of Muḥammed 'Alī (1805-1849) who managed to set up a dynasty

---

[1] The period of the *Nahḍah* is hard to delimit, especially with regard to Lebanon, where there is a tendency to include any author who wrote Arabic without too many mistakes. Ǧarmānūs Farḥāt (1670-1732), who composed an Arabic grammar, is commonly included. Some include also Aḥmad al-Barbīr (1747-1811) and Niqūlā al-Turk (1763-1828) on the strength of the *maqāmāt* they composed. Louis Cheikho considered the chronogram as belonging to the period of the revival, which is too much honour for this sort of artistry. An early attempt to provide a definition was made by Ǧ. Zaydān in his *Ta'rīkh Ādāb al-lughah al-'Arabiyyah*, vol. 4, p. 16 (Cairo, n.d., new edition revised and annotated by Dr. Shawqī Ḍayf). There he enumerates the following characteristics : 1. The establishment of new schools, 2. (The introduction of) printing presses, 3. (The introduction of) journalism, 4. The spirit of personal freedom, 5. (The establishment of) literary and learned freedom, 6. (The foundation of) public libraries, 7. (The foundation of) museums, 8. (The foundation of) theaters, 9. The interest of Europeans in Arabic literature.

[2] The Golden Period can be taken as coinciding with the passing of the caliphate from the Umayyads to the Abassids until the Seljuqs entered Baghdad, or from 750-1055 A.D. So H. A. R. Gibb, *Arabic Literature*. Oxford, 1963², p. 46-116.

after the French withdrawal and who eventually extended his sway over Palestine and Syria (1831-1840) as well. The movement, if we may say so, did not gain momentum until after the Druze insurrection in Lebanon and after Ismāʿīl's accession to the Egyptian throne in 1863. In America the first signs of a new Arabic literature were seen in the first decade of the twentieth century.

Largely parallel to the regional diversity of Egypt, Lebanon and North America, runs a line separating Muslims and Christians. In Egypt the *Nahḍah* was by and large a Muslim affair until the migration of Christian Lebanese intellectuals and semi-intellectuals widened the scene. In Lebanon and in North America the Christians were leading the revival.

The religious persuasion is significant because Christians were familiar with other types of poetry than were current among the Muslims. The Book of Psalms and other poetical parts of the Bible opened for the Christians wider vistas of poetry than traditional Arab poetry was offering[3]. However, to effect a change requires more than a disposition. The circumstances must favour the change and a creative personality is needed to translate all this into action. With regard to circumstances it is not remarkable that the most far-reaching breaks with the Arabic literary tradition occurred among the Christian Lebanese emigrants in America. Their intimacy with other literatures than Arabic must have given them a sense of relativity with respect to the literary products of their own language. Apart from new ideas they were ready to accept new forms, which they had found in the Western literatures.

Returning to the beginning of the *Nahḍah*, it has to be asserted that among all the influences and barriers, such as the confrontation with Western culture, Turkish rule, Western colonialism, Muslim and Christian beliefs, the introduction of the printing-press occupies a place of its own in the development of modern Arabic literature.

Long before the nineteenth century, printing-presses with Arabic founts had already been installed in Lebanon, but their output was restricted in the main to a few religious tracts and to Psalters. Bonaparte's press, confiscated in Rome and brought to Egypt in 1797 was used for communiqués in Arabic [4]. Apart from a treatise on smallpox this press issued nothing of interest for the local population [5]. The French,

---

[3] S. Moreh, "Poetry in Prose (*al-Shiʿr al-Manthūr*) in Modern Arabic Literature". *Middle Eastern Studies*, vol. 4, 4 (July 1968), p. 330-360.

[4] J. Heyworth-Dunne, *An Introduction to the History of Education in Modern Egypt*. London, 1968², p. 99. Ğurgī Zaydān, *Taʾrīkh Ādāb al-lughah al-ʿArabiyyah*, vol. 4, p. 46.

[5] J. Heyworth-Dunne, "Printing and Translation under Muhammad ʿAlī of Egypt. The foundation

however, set an example. Moreover, they had made an indelible impression by defeating the Mameluks who had governed Egypt ever since 1250, and who had remained the ruling elite after the Turkish conquest in 1517. Muḥammed 'Alī, selfstyled ruler of Egypt from 1805 onward [6], wanted to modernize his army on European lines and attracted European instructors for that purpose. At the same time he sent Egyptians to Italy at first, and later to France, to be trained in various skills [7]. The art of printing was learnt in Rome, from where the well-known Būlāq-press was brought to Cairo in 1821 [8].

The returns of Muḥammad 'Alī's missions to Europe were slow to come. The low educational standards of many of the students who were sent abroad and the arbitrary use of them after their return limited the effect of these missions [9]. Only few of the students were outstanding, such as Rifā'ah Rāfi' al-Ṭahṭāwī, the Imām of the first group of students in France, who, among other things, qualified himself as an able translator [10]. He founded the School of Languages (*Madrasat al-Alsun*) in 1835, to which he added a translation office in 1841. In this way he provided Egypt with a number of capable translators and with the translations of foreign works necessary in the newly established schools and training colleges. Though these translations do

---

of modern Arabic". *JRAS*, 1940, p. 327. Heyworth-Dunne, *An Introduction to the History of Education in Modern Egypt*. p. 99.

[6] 'Abd al-Raḥmān al-Ǧabartī (1754-1822), *Ta'rīkh 'Aǧā'ib al-Āthār fī al-tarāǧim wa al-akhbār* (first impression Cairo, 1290 H/1876 A.D., recently republished by Dār al-Fāris, Beirut, n.d.), II 540-III 74, chronicles the events of Muḥammad 'Alī's rise to power. French translation, *Merveilles biographiques et historiques ou Chronique du Cheikh Abd-el-Rahman el Djabarti*, Vol. VII, Cairo, 1892, pp. 128-383.

[7] Heyworth-Dunne, *An Introduction to the History of Education in Modern Egypt*. Until 1818 twenty-eight students were sent to Europe (p. 106). For the period between 1818 and 1826 no records are available (p. 106). Between 1826 and 1837 a total number of 152 students went abroad (lists of names on p. 159-163 and p. 170-175). From 1837 until the end of Muḥammad 'Alī's reign another 36 students went to Europe (p. 222). (E. F.) Jomard, "École égyptienne de Paris" *Nouveau Journal Asiatique*, Tome II (août 1828), p. 96-117).

[8] Al-Fīkūnt Fīlīb di Ṭarrāzī, *Ta'rīkh al-Ṣiḥāfah al-'Arabiyyah*, I (History of the Arabic Press), Beirut, 1923, p. 49. The press received its name from the small town Būlāq, now a district of Cairo, where it was installed.

[9] Anouar Louca, *Voyageurs et écrivains égyptiens en France au XIX*[e] *siècle*. Paris, 1970, p. 48 ff., quoting a.o. P. N. Hamont, *L'Égypte sous Méhémet Ali*. Paris, 1843, pp. 194 ff. The latter's criticism of Muḥammad 'Alī's rule does not seem wholly unbiased. It was characterized as "le fruit d'une déception" by Jean-Marie Carré, *Voyageurs et écrivains français en Égypte*, Vol. I. *Du début à la fin de la domination turque (1517-1840)*, Le Caire, 1932, p. 289 f.

[10] Louca, *Voyageurs et écrivains*, p. 54 et Première Partie, Ch. II, p. 55-74. Cf. Prince 'Umar Ṭūsūn, *Al-ba'athāt al-'ilmiyyah fī 'ahd Muḥammad 'Alī, thumma fī 'ahday 'Abbās al-Awwal wa Sa'īd*. Alexandria, 1934, p. 46. Cf. also J. Heyworth-Dunne, "Rifa'a Badawi Rafi' al-Tahtawi, the Egyptian Revivalist" *BSOS* IX (1939), p. 961 ff., X (1940), pp. 399 ff. A. A. Badawī, *Rifā'ah al-Ṭahṭāwī Bik*. Cairo, 1950.

not concern literary works, they were important for the development of Arabic literature in that they created a new style.

After Muḥammad 'Alī had been forced by the great powers to leave Syria in 1840 a cultural decline set in, which continued under his successors 'Abbās I (1849-1854) and Sa'īd (1854-63)[11]. Ismā'īl (1863-1879), who had studied in France for some time, offered new opportunities. In these years the first learned periodical in Arabic the *Rawḍat al-Madāris* (The Schoolyard), founded by 'Alī Mubārak in 1870, was edited by al-Ṭahṭāwī. The latter also ventured into the field of literature by translating Fénélon's Télémaque[12], which is possibly the first translation into Arabic in modern times of a foreign literary work.

Different from Egypt, the stimulus of the cultural awakening in Lebanon did not issue from the personal ambitions of the ruler, but to a large extent from the proselytizing force of Western, mainly American, Presbyterian missionaries.

American Protestant missionaries came to Beirut in 1823[13], and in 1831 the Jesuits returned. The first two American missionaries to arrive in Beirut functioned within the framework of planned missionary activities in the Holy Land, and especially in Jerusalem. They stayed in Beirut because the Eastern Churches had adopted a hostile attitude towards the missionaries, and because of the tension occasioned by the Greek revolt in 1821, which made residence in a harbour city preferable to a landlocked place[14]. In 1825 their number was strengthened by the arrival of Dr. Eli

---

[11] Heyworth-Dunne, *An Introduction to the History of Education in Modern Egypt*, pp. 287 and 301. Louca, *Voyageurs et écrivains*, p. 101, does not think very highly of the cultural efforts of 'Abbās I. This successor of Muḥammad 'Alī is characterized by him as a man who abhorred popular education. Louca's appreciation of Sa'īd is not better, describing the student's mission to France during his rule as acts of generosity which had nothing to do with a high policy of education, nor with a felt need for specialists in certain fields. Heyworth-Dunne, on the other hand, states "that many of Muḥammad 'Alī's innovations owed their origin to an artificial situation, and that, if 'Abbās put an end to some of them, he did so out of sheer common sense which is credited to him by more than one writer" (*An Introduction to the History of Education in Modern Egypt*, p. 289). Sa'īd, on the contrary, is described as "careless, impetuous, extravagant and unstable" (p. 313). Brockelmann, GAL II², p. 623, writes that Muḥammad 'Alī's first successor already felt compelled to end the monopolies and the most exacting taxes, and to put limits on the army and fleet. The situation of the people became still more tolerable under Sa'īd.

[12] The translation was made in 1849 but not published before 1869 in Beirut (so Abdel-Aziz Abdel-Meguid, *The Modern Arabic Short Story, its emergence, development and form*). Cairo, n.d., p. 64.

[13] A. L. Tibawi, "The American Missionaries in Beirut and Buṭrus al-Bustānī", *Middle Eastern Affairs*, Number 3 (St. Antony's Papers, Number 16). London, 1963, p. 144.

[14] A. L. Tibawi, "The American Missionaries in Beirut and Buṭrus al-Bustānī", *Middle Eastern Affairs*, Number 3, p. 144.

Smith, who gave the mission an enormous impetus establishing schools and extending aid to existing ones [15].

The American missionaries were supported by a printing press, which had been brought to Malta in 1822 [16]. In 1830 an Arabic fount was added to the plant, but no Arabic books came from this press until after its transfer to Beirut [17]. The Jesuits, in their turn, established schools and set up their own printing press in 1848 [18], now known as the Imprimerie Catholique. In 1875 they established the Université Saint Joseph [19] after the American missionaries had created their University in 1866, now known as American University of Beirut [20].

The American missionaries found Lebanese collaborators, among whom Nāṣīf al-Yāziǧī (1800-1871) and Buṭrus al-Bustānī (1819-1883) were outstanding. Nāṣīf al-Yāziǧī composed a number of books on Arabic grammar and on logic and medicine for use in the classroom. His *Maqāmāt*, the *Mağma' al-Baḥrayn* (The Confluence of the Two Seas), in which he emulated Badī' al-Zamān al-Hamadhānī (d. 1007) and al-Ḥarīrī (d. 1122), are mnemotechnic exercises rather than literary creations [21]. This is not surprising for a man whose knowledge of the language must be rated far higher than his literary abilities. His poetry is traditional and mediocre [22], and his commentary on the tenth-century poet al-Mutannabī [23] stresses, in the traditional way, the linguistic rather than the literary merits of this poet. He was the first Lebanese in modern times to give so much attention to language training, a long neglected

---

[15] A. L. Tibawi, "The American Missionaries in Beirut and Buṭrus al-Bustānī", *Middle Eastern Affairs*, Number 3, p. 149.

[16] A. L. Tibawi, *American Interests in Syria, 1800-1901. A Study of Educational, Literary and Religious Work*. Oxford, Clarendon Press, 1966, p. 52.

[17] A. L. Tibawi, *American Interests in Syria, 1800-1901*", p. 71.

[18] L. Cheikho, *Al-Ādāb al-'Arabiyyah fī al-qarn al-tāsi' 'ashar* (Arabic Literature in the 19th Century), I, Beirut, 1924², p. 48.

[19] L. Cheikho, *Al-Ādāb al-'Arabiyyah fī al-qarn al-tāsi' 'ashar*, II Beirut, 1926², p. 4.

[20] About the American University of Beirut cf. S. B. L. Penrose, *That They May Have Life. The Story of the American University of Beirut*, 1866-1941. New York, 1941, and B. Dodge, *The American University of Beirut*, Beirut, 1958.

[21] *Maqāmāt* or episodes are anecdotal stories around one central figure. They are usually written in rhymed prose in which the majority of words rhyme one by one or in parallel clauses. Cf. A. F. L. Beeston, "The Genesis of the *Maqāmāt* Genre", *Journal of Arabic Literature*, II, 1971, p. 1-12. The *Mağma' al-Baḥrayn* was first published Beirut, 1856 (See Y. A. Dāghir, *Maṣādir al-Dirāsah al-Adabiyyah* (Sources for Literary Study), part 2, Beirut, 1955, p. 755).

[22] The first part of this *dīwān* was published, Beirut, 1852, the second part followed in 1864 and the third part in 1883 also in Beirut (Cf. Dāghir, *Maṣādir*, II, p. 755).

[23] The title of this work is *Al-'Urf al-ṭayyib fī sharḥ Dīwān Abī al-Ṭayyib* which could be taken to mean "A Good Plain Language to explain the *Dīwān* of Abū Ṭayyib (al-Mutanabbī)".

field among the Christians [24]. In doing so he laid the bases for the Lebanese literary *Nahḍah.*

Al-Bustānī was more of a literary man than al-Yāziğī. Witness to this are the periodicals he issued in collaboration with his son Salīm. He established the weekly *al-Ğinān* (The Gardens), and his son founded *al-Ğannah* (The Garden) which was discontinued after two years [25]. He enriched Arabic philology with an Arabic dictionary *Muḥīṭ al-Muḥīṭ* (The Circumference of the Ocean), abridged by himself in the *Quṭr al Muḥīṭ* (The Diameter of the Ocean) [26]. On his own he began to write the first Arabic encyclopedia *Dā'irat al-Ma'ārif* (The Circle of Sciences, Beirut 1876 and after), of which eight volumes appeared during his lifetime [27]. At the request of the American missionaries he also translated *Robinson Crusoe* [28]. Additionally at the request of the missionaries, Nāṣīf al-Yāziğī and Buṭrus al-Bustānī prepared an Arabic translation of the Bible in close co-operation with two of the missionaries, Eli Smith and Cornelius van Dyck [29]. This translation was soon followed by the so-called Jesuit-Bible prepared by Nāṣīf al-Yāziğī's son Ibrāhīm (1847-1906) [30]. Both translations were written in a careful style, more simple than the ornate form of Arabic considered adequate for a work of art, but at the same time not undistinguished and at a far remove from the sometimes crude styles of the newspapers.

Last not least, the son of Buṭrus al-Bustānī, Sulaymān (1856-1925) enriched Arabic literature with a translation of the *Iliad*, using multiple rhymes and different metres in the various parts instead of the usual mono-rhyme and one-metre poems [31].

In Egypt, Ismā'īl's ambitious programs created a favourable atmosphere for creative enterprises. The British occupation brought Sir Evelyn Baring, later Earl of Cromer, to Egypt. He upheld press-freedom throughout his period of office (1882-1907) [32]. This atmosphere attracted members of the Lebanese intelligentsia who resented the

---

24 Cf. Khalil S. Hawi, *Kahlil Gibran*, p. 33.

25 Cheikho, *al-Ādāb al-'Arabiyyah fī al-qarn al-tāsi' 'ashar*, II, p. 6.

26 Both editions were published in Beirut in 1870 (cf. Dāghir, *Maṣādir*, II, p. 180 ff.

27 Cheikho, *al-Ādāb al-'Arabiyyah fī al-qarn al-tāsi' 'ashar*, I, p. 127.

28 The Arabic title chosen by al-Bustānī is : *Kitāb al-tuḥfah al-Bustāniyyah fī al-asfār al-karūziyyah*, Beirut, 1861. (From A. L. Tibawi, "The American Missionaries in Beirut and Buṭrus al-Bustānī", *Middle Eastern Affairs*, Number 3, p. 170, note 114). The American missionaries seem to have estimated *Robinson Crusoe* very highly. Already in 1835, A. L. Tibawi writes in the same note, an Arabic edition left the Malta press.

29 Cheikho, *al-Ādāb al-'Arabiyyah fī al-qarn al-tāsi' 'ashar*, I, p. 80.

30 Cheikho, *al-Ādāb al-'Arabiyyah fī al-qarn al-tāsi' 'ashar*, II, p. 39.

31 First edition, Cairo, 1904 (Dāghir, *Maṣādir*, II, 190).

32 The Earl of Cromer, *Modern Egypt*. 2 vols. London, 1908. Mounah A. Khoury, *Poetry and the Making of Modern Egypt*, Leiden, 1971, p. 42, 81 and 165.

restrictions of the Turkish authorities or, for other reasons were prepared to leave their country of birth. Successes of some must have attracted others.

Notable émigrés were Dr. Yaʿqūb Ṣarrūf and Dr. Fāris Nimr, who took their learned journal *al-Muqtaṭaf* in 1884 to Egypt. The Turks had nothing to do with their departure, it seems. These two distinguished Arabs were on the staff of the American University of Beirut from which they were dismissed in 1884 [33] in the course of something like an anti-Darwinist purge. Another émigré of note was Ǧirǧī Zaydān who founded the cultural and literary monthly *al-Hilāl* (The Crescent) in 1892 [34].

On the whole, the Lebanese formed the front-rank in the development of the periodical press in Egypt. Their skill in editing dailies and magazines may be partly due to the examples set by their European and American co-religionists, whom religious zeal had brought to Lebanon. The communalistic structure of the Lebanese population, characterized by a great number of religious minorities each having its own newspaper, may have kept a spirit of competition alive with all its negative and positive implications. Whatever may have been the cause of this skill, a fact is that the well-known daily *al-Ahrām* (The Antiquities, the Pyramids) was founded by Lebanese émigrés in 1876 [35]. Dr. Yaʿqūb Ṣarrūf and Dr. Fāris Nimr edited their own daily *al-Muqaṭṭam* (name of the hills east of Cairo) from 1889 onward [36].

One of the consequences of the growth of the periodical press was that the poet was henceforth confronted with a different kind of audience. Even his praise of the ruler was no longer restricted to a small court circle, but could obtain the approval or disapproval of far wider groups. This eventually led to a less complicated language and to a gradual diminution of archaic words in which Arab poets had revelled until then. Many poets, however, remained addicted to a sonorous language in which archaisms played a vital part. Another result of the fast growing press was that a poet and an author could enjoy a fame of unprecedented extent in their own lifetime.

The precursor of the literary revival in Egypt, Maḥmūd Sāmī al-Bārūdī (1839-1904), did not enjoy such fame. Being banished to Ceylon from 1882-1900 as an accomplice in the ʿUrābī insurrection of 1882, he had little or no opportunity to have his poems published in the columns of the dailies or in the magazines [37]. Most of his poems were

---

[33] Nadia Farag, "The Lewis Affair and the Fortunes of al-Muqtaṭaf", *Middle Eastern Studies*, Vol. 8, 1 (January 1972), p. 73-83.

[34] Cf. the biographical note in Zaydān's *Ta'rīkh Ādāb al-Lughah al-ʿArabiyyah*, part 4, Cairo, n.d., p. 283-285 (New impression revised and annotated by Dr. Shawqī Ḍayf).

[35] M. Hartmann, *The Arabic Press of Egypt*. London, 1899, p. 10.

[36] M. Hartmann, *The Arabic Press of Egypt*. London, 1899, p. 11.

[37] M. A. Khoury, *Poetry and the Making of Modern Egypt*, p. 44 f.

posthumously published from manuscripts. Part of his work had found its way into *al-Wasīlah al-adabiyyah ilā al-'ulūm al-'arabiyyah* (The Literary Approach to the Sciences of the Arabic Language) an anthology compiled by Ḥusayn al-Marṣafī (2 volumes, Cairo 1878-1881). Bārūdī himself compiled an anthology of Arabic verse during his exile in Ceylon. With it he fostered an interest in the poets of the so-called Golden Period instead of the poets of the Silver Period, who were in favour at that time [38].

Later poets, such as Aḥmad Shawqī (1869-1932) and Ḥāfiẓ Ibrāhīm (1870-1932), could make use of the opportunities offered by the press. Shawqī's poetry, especially, was much in demand. Muḥammad Ṣabrī, who collected the scattered poems of Shawqī found more than 5000 poems not included in the complete works [39]. Shawqī innovated, as far as the subjects of his verses were concerned, but on the strength of his style he is counted among the neo-classicists. The quality of the poetry of both Shawqī and Ḥāfiẓ Ibrāhīm, as well as their popularity, made it difficult for modernizers to come through [40].

One of the moderns was the Syrian émigré Khalīl Muṭrān (1872-1949), who was influenced by the French romantics, though the precise sources of his inspiration are difficult to determine [41]. He stands on his own against the English inspired modernists such as 'Abd al-Raḥmān Shukrī (1886-1958), 'Abbās Maḥmūd al-'Aqqād (1889-1964) and Ibrāhīm 'Abd al-Qādir al-Māzinī (1890-1947). They admired the English romantics, such as Shelley, Wordsworth and Coleridge, and they advocated a poetry of emotion. At the same time they insisted on the purity of the language; adhered to the monorhyme; and remained by and large, within the limits of traditional Arabic meters [42]. They worked closely together for some time until Shukrī discovered and exposed al-Māzinī as having passed off translations of English poems as his own [43]. Al-Māzinī, in turn, ridiculed Shukrī's verses and this may have caused the latter, a sensitive and gifted poet, to give up writing poetry [44]. Al-'Aqqād continued his

---

[38] The Silver Period is usually taken to be the period from about 1000 until the sacking of Baghdad by the Mongols in 1258. Cf. H. A. R. Gibb, *Arabic Literature,* Oxford, 1963², p. 117-140.

[39] Muḥammad Ṣabrī, *Al-Shawqiyyāt al-Mağhūlah* (The Unknown Poems of Shawqī, 2 vols. Cairo, 1961-2) (Cf. M. A. Khoury, *Poetry and the Making of Modern Egypt*, p. 44).

[40] Cf. what M. A. Khoury writes about Shukrī's attempts to innovate. *Poetry and the Making of Modern Egypt*, Leiden, 1971, p. 182 f.

[41] Cf. Muḥammad Mandūr, *Muḥāḍarāt 'an Khalīl Muṭrān*. Cairo, 1954.

[42] About the purity of the language see al-'Aqqād's preface to *al-Ghirbāl*, p. 5-12.

[43] 'Abd al-Raḥmān Shukrī, *Dīwān*. Complete edition, Alexandria, 1960 (Introduction to the fifth part, originally published in 1916), p. 373.

[44] Ibrāhīm 'Abd al-Qādir al-Māzinī, "Ṣanam al-Alā'īb" (Idol of the Playthings) I and II in: 'Abbās Maḥmūd al-'Aqqād and Ibrāhīm 'Abd al-Qādir al-Māzinī, *Al-Dīwān*, Cairo, third impression, n.d. p. 57-73 and 177-190. Only the second part has been signed by al-Māzinī.

co-operation with al-Māzinī, and this resulted in *al-Dīwān*, a collection of literary essays published in two fascicles. Al-Māzinī wrote about Shukrī's poetry in these essays. Al-ʿAqqād, on the other hand, turned against Aḥmad Shawqī, chaffing him for lack of unity of his poems [45].

The innovations introduced into Arabic poetry in Lebanon itself were few. Poets like Nasīb Arslān (1868-1934), Ilyās Fayyāḍ (1879-1930) and Bishārah al-Khūrī (1883-1968) were not less traditional than the neo-classicist poets of Egypt. Bishārah al-Khūrī demonstrated with his pen-name al-Akhṭal al-ṣaghīr (al-Akhṭal the Younger) his preference for the poetry of the Christian poet al-Akhṭal (c. 710), the *protégé* of the Umayyad caliph ʿAbd al-Malik (685-705), residing in Damascus.

More drastic innovations in Arabic literature took place in America, where a large Lebanese colony had been formed in the decades around the turn of the century. The masses of the Arabophone migrants soon made it worthwhile to publish Arabic newspapers, the first of which, *Kawkab Amīrkā* (The Star of America), appeared in New York, dated 5 *Nīsān* (April), 1892 [46]. Other papers followed and in a short time every religious community had its own platform [47]. These papers and their printers provided the technical means for the development of Arabic literature among the emigrants. This literature entered upon an interesting phase, when, shortly after the turn of the century, new poetic forms were being practised. The poets who wrote this new poetry were all of Christian origin and, therefore, they could abandon the traditional concept of poetry more easily than their Muslim brethern. Second, most of them had not enjoyed the luxury of a thorough education in the Arabic language, to say nothing about the prosodiacal knowledge a poet had to have. No wonder that they introduced new subjects, and wrote poetry in a new style. Their common experience of a long journey overseas; of being separated from one's kith and kin, and from one's familiar surroundings; was reflected in their writings.

They were not dogmatic, were anticlerical and had democratic feelings. The so-called *shiʿr manthūr* (Poetry in Prose) in the fashion of Walt Whitman, may be considered an expression of their anti-dogmatism [48]. Ǧibrān Khalīl Ǧibrān (1883-1932) was

---

[45] Al-ʿAqqād, "Shawqī fī al-mīzān" (Shawqī in the balance), in: al-ʿAqqād and al-Māzinī, *Al-Dīwān*, pp. 5-11 and 115-127.

[46] Al-Fīkūnt Fīlīb dī Ṭarrāzī, *Ta'rīkh al-Ṣiḥāfah al-ʿArabiyyah* (History of the Arabic Press), I, Beirut, 1913, p. 33.

[47] Nuʿaymah, *Sabʿūn. Ḥikāyat ʿUmr. Al-Marḥalah al-thāniyah* (Seventy. A Life Story. The Second Stage), Beirut, 1964², p. 69.

[48] Cf. S. Moreh, "Poetry in Prose (*al-Shiʿr al-manthūr*) in Modern Arabic Literature", *Middle Eastern Studies*, Vol. 4, 4 (July, 1968), p. 330-360.

probably the first to write this kind of poetry, in 1904 [49], closely followed by Amīn al-Rayḥānī (1876-1940), who published his first poems in prose in 1905. Nu'aymah, on the other hand, did not practice this kind of poetry. Different from both Ǧibrān and al-Rayḥānī, he wrote stanzaic poetry using multiple rhymes. His poems are contemplative and almost all have to do with questions of conscience and with his pantheistic beliefs [50].

In 1920 a group of poets and authors, among them Ǧibrān and Nu'aymah, organized themselves into *al-Rābiṭah al-qalamiyyah* with the express aim of lending more weight to the reforms they advocated. It is quite possible that the harsh criticism to which their products were subjected, especially in Egypt, together with their search for literary recognition, helped in bringing them together. Like the poets of the *dīwān*-group [51] in Egypt, they wanted poetry to be emotional, but they differed with that group in their appreciation of the rules of the prosody. They allowed the poet considerable, if not total, freedom from these rules or, at any rate, relegated them to a secondary place, having significance for the literary level of the poem but not as evidence of it being poetry or not [52]. This, certainly, was a reversal of the common practice.

As regards prose, the Arabs were never short of story-tellers, historians, geographers and preachers, all of whom seem to have had a special feeling for the anecdote. Peculiar to the Arabs was the *maqāmah* (Episode), an anecdotal story about a sympathetic scoundrel who readily enters any dispute and always leaves the arena a victor. The genre was invented by Badī' al-Zamān al-Hamadhānī (968-1007) and continued in a masterly way by al-Ḥarīrī (1054-1122). The rich vocabulary with rare words in abundance; the metaphors; the symmetry in clauses and sentences; the lavish use of rhyme-words; made the collections esteemed textbooks for language

[49] S. Moreh, "Poetry in Prose (*al-Shi'r al-manthūr*) in Modern Arabic Literature", *Middle Eastern Studies*, Vol. 4, 4, p. 335.

[50] S. Moreh, "Poetry in Prose ...", p. 337. The poetry of Amīn al-Rayḥānī, in part published in his *al-Rayḥāniyyāt*, volume 2 (Beirut, 1910), p. 182-233 and volume 4 (Beirut, 1924), p. 3-79, has been collected in one volume *Hutāf al-awdiyah* (The Cry of the Wadis), Beirut, 1955. The poems have not been included in *al-Rayḥāniyyāt* in two volumes compiled by Albert al-Rayḥānī from the original *al-Rayḥāniyyāt* with the addition of otherwise not collected writings.

[51] The *dīwān* group is considered to consist of 'Abd al-Raḥmān Shukrī, 'Abbas Maḥmūd al-'Aqqād and Ibrāhīm 'Abd al-Qādir al-Māzinī, even though the book *al-Dīwān* from which their name is derived, was published after Shukrī had left the group. Cf. A. M. K. Al-Zubaidi, "The Dīwān School", *Journal of Arabic Literature*, Vol. I, Leiden, 1970, p. 36-48.

[52] So Nu'aymah, "Al-Maqāyīs al-adabiyyah" (The literary yardsticks), *Al-Ghirbāl*, 1964[7], p. 65-74.

training. This last aspect seems to have been appreciated by men like Nāṣīf al-Yāziǧī, whose *maqāmāt* have previously been mentioned [53].

A drawback of the *maqāmah*-genre is that it is too laborious and too intricate to reach large audiences. The genre soon lapsed into disuse before the onrush of the Western-styled story. One of the last notable *maqāmah*-writers in Egypt was Muḥammad al-Muwayliḥī, the author of *Ḥadīth ʿĪsā Ibn Hishām* (The Story of ʿIsā son of Hishām, Cairo, 1906) [54].

The success of the story comes fully to the credit of the daily and periodical press. One of the first papers to publish stories, translated or original, was Bustānī's *Ǧinān* (The Gardens) [55]. Buṭrus' son Salīm made his début with his story *Ramyah min ghayr rāmin* (An Unintended Hit) [56]. He contributed many stories to his father's paper and also wrote serials, among which may be mentioned the historical novel *Zanūbīyā malikat Tadmūr* (Zaynobia, Queen of Tadmor) in 1871.

Stories became so popular that even their most declared opponents had to accept them. *Al-Mashriq*, edited by Father Louis Cheikho, S.J. in Beirut from 1898 onward, published stories with a moral or religious tenor [57]. *Al-Muqtaṭaf* began to exhort educators to give the youth useful things to read to divert them from reading stories, which, as a genre, the paper judged demoralizing. In 1886, however, this same paper promised its readers a translated novel, provided they paid their subscription fees for the coming year in January 1887 [58]. The success of the story gave rise to special magazines, the first of which *Silsilat al-Fukāhāt* (Chain of Funny Stories) appeared in Beirut, 1884 [59].

In America Amīn al-Rayḥānī and Khalīl Ǧibrān were the first to write stories of some literary value. Being removed from the Lebanese scene they could use these

---

[53] Cf. above p. 5.

[54] Recent research on this work was done by R. Allen, *Muḥammad al-Muwayliḥī, A Study of Hadīth ʿĪsā ibn Hishām.* Albany, N. Y., 1974 (microfiche edition, 899 pp. on 10 sheets). Earlier he had published an article on the same subject : R. Allen, "*Hadīth ʿĪsā Ibn Hisham* by Muhammad al-Muwailihī. A Reconsideration", *Journal of Arabic Literature*, Vol. I (1970), p. 88-108.

[55] Muḥammad Yūsuf Naǧm, *Al-Qiṣṣah fī al-adab al-ʿarabī al-ḥadīth* (The Narrative in Modern Arabic Literature), 1780-1914, Beirut, 1966³, p. 41 ff.

[56] The text of this story is published by Abdel-Aziz Abdel-Meguid, *The Modern Arabic Short Story. Its emergences, Development, and Form*, Cairo, n.d., Arabic section, p. 5-9. See also English section, p. 78.

[57] Abdel-Aziz Abdel-Meguid, *The Modern Arabic Short Story*, p. 82.

[58] Muḥammad Yūsuf Naǧm, *Al-Qiṣṣah fī al-adab al-ʿarabi al-ḥadīth* (The Narrative in Modern Arabic Literature), 1780-1914, Beirut, 1966³, p. 17 f.

[59] Naǧm, *Al-Qiṣṣah fī al-adab al-ʿarabī al-ḥadīth*, Beirut, 1966³, p. 20.

stories to vent their criticisms against those in power in Lebanese society. The clergy, especially, came under their attacks. Al-Rayḥānī did this in his parable *al-Muḥālafah al-thulāthiyyah fī al-mamlakah al-Ḥayawāniyyah* (The Triple Alliance in the Animal Kingdom, New York, 1903) and so did Ğibrān in his *'Arā'is al-murūğ* (Nymphs of the Valley, New York, 1907) and in his *al-Arwāḥ al-mutamarridah* (Souls Rebellious, New York, 1908). In the first volume he also broached the question of reincarnation, making the same lovers meet in 116 B.C. and in 1890 A.D. in Baalbeck. Ğibrān's stories were very sentimental and a little highfalutin. Nu'aymah, on the other hand, was far more sober. His thorough acquaintance with Russian literature, as well as with English literature made him a unique personality in Arabic speaking circles. His stories were close-knit in comparison to what had been written so far. Moreover, he was one of the first Arab writers to care for the psychological development of the characters [60].

The novel took a longer time to develop. Though the first serialized novels appeared from 1870 onward [61], and although Ğirğī Zaydān began to write his historical novels from 1892 onwards the first Egyptian narrative deserving the name "novel" is generally taken to be *Zaynab*, by Ḥusayn Haykal (Paris, 1913) [62]. Other predecessors of Haykal were Farah Anṭūn [63] and Ya'qūb Ṣarrūf [64]. Khalīl Ğibrān saw his *al-Ağniḥah al-mutakassirah* (Broken Wings) come off the press in New York in 1908. Amīn al-Rayḥānī published his *Zanbaqat al-ghawr* (The Lily of the Depth) New York, 1915, followed by his *Khāriğ al-ḥarīm* (Outside the Harem) New York, 1917 [65]. Mikhā'īl Nu'aymah started a novel in 1917. Four instalments appeared in *al-Funūn* [66], but then the author had to break off because of the war. This novel, with a few alterations in the existing parts, was completed and published in 1948.

---

60 Cf. Chapter IV.

61 Nağm, *Al-Qiṣṣah fī al-adab al-'arabī al-ḥadīth,* p. 43 names Salīm al-Bustānī (1848-1884) as the author of the serialized novel *al-Hiyām fī ğinān al-Shām* (Passionate Love in the Gardens of Damascus), cf. also Y. S. Dāghir, *Maṣādir* II, p. 187.

62 H. A. R. Gibb, "Studies in Contemporary Arabic Literature", IV, "The Egyptian Novel", *BSOS* VII, 1 (London, 1933), p. 1-22. Republished in *Studies on the Civilization of Islam*, London, 1962, p. 286-303. For the date of publication of this novel see Hamdi Sakkut, *The Egyptian Novel and its Main Trends, 1913-1952,* Cairo, 1971, p. 12.

63 Faraḥ Anṭūn wrote a.o. the historical novel *Ūrushalīm al-ğadīdah aw fatḥ al-'arab Bayt al-Maqdis* (New Jerusalem or the Arab Conquest of the House of Holiness), Alexandria, 1904. Cf. Nağm, *Al-Qiṣṣah fī al-adab al-'arabī al-ḥadīth,* p. 208-211.

64 Ya'qūb Ṣarrūf wrote a.o. *Fatāt Miṣr* (Cairene Girl) in 1905 and his *Fatāt Fayyūm* (Fayyum Girl) in 1908.

65 Cf. Ğamīl Ğabr, *Amīn al-Rayḥānī,* n.pl., n.d. Foreword dated 1 Jan. 1948, pp. 62 and 66. *Khāriğ al-ḥarīm* (Outside the Harem), moreover is advertised as being for sale in a 1917 edition of *Zanbaqat al-ghawr,* by Sharikat al-Funūn, New York.

66 Cf. Chapter IV, footnote 4.

On the whole the novel had a fragile existence in Arabic literature until recently. The contribution of the Lebanese émigrés to the genre remained limited, which may be due to financial as well as to other reasons. As can be gleaned from the experiences with the first *Mağmūʿah* (Collection) of *al-Rābiṭah al-qalamiyyah* (The Pen League), New York in 1919, the Arabs in America were not in the habit of buying books, whereas the prices of Arabic books published in America, were prohibitive in the Arab countries [67].

The periodical press also encouraged prose forms other than fiction. The most notable of these was the essay or the article. One of the first to excell in this kind of literature was Fāris al-Shidyāq of Lebanese Christian origin (1804-1887). In 1855 he published in Paris a volume with the title *al-Sāq ʿalā al-sāq fī mā huwa al-fāryāq* (With Crossed Legs about Fār(is al-Shid)yāq). These texts are generally considered to be *maqāmāt*, but they display features which remind us of the essay and the story. In Egypt Qāsim Amīn (1856-1908), the author of *Taḥrīr al-mar'ah* (The Liberation of Women, Cairo, 1899), which may be considered the starting point of the emancipation of women in Egypt, was one of the first to compose essays. Another essayist of note was Muṣṭafā Luṭfī al-Manfalūṭī (1872-1924), who published his *Naẓarāt* (Opinions) from 1907 onward in the paper *al-Mu'ayyad* (The Authorized) in Cairo [68]. In his essays he dealt with the social evils of European civilization, and with the defence of Islam. However, al-Mafalūṭī was not a front-line reformer. In this respect he was easily outpaced by Muḥammad ʿAbduh (1849-1905) and his disciple Rashīd Riḍā (1865-1925) as far as the Islamic religion was concerned, and by Aḥmad Luṭfī al-Sayyid (1872-1963) who devoted his attention to matters of social importance. He also opened his newspaper *al-Ğarīdah* (The Newspaper [69], issued from 1907-1914) to the new literary movement, which included Muḥammad Ḥusayn Haykal and ʿAbd al-Raḥmān Shukrī.

The Lebanese in America went their own way. Amīn al-Rayḥānī's first essay, published in the New York newspaper *al-Hudā* (The Right Course) in 1902, deals with the French revolution [70]. Ğibrān's earliest essay deals with some Arabian musical instruments. Nuʿaymah practised the literary essay in which he said some fundamental things. Some of his essays are real manifestoes of the new literary movement in America [71]. In due time, however, he turned into a new, non-literary direction : he

---

[67] Nuʿaymah, *Sabʿūn* (Seventy). Vol. II, Beirut, 1964², p. 165.

[68] Cf. H. A. R. Gibb, "Studies in Contemporary Arabic Literature" II, "Manfaluti and the New Style", *Studies on the Civilization of Islam*, London, 1962, p. 258-268.

[69] H. A. R. Gibb, "Studies in Contemporary Arabic Literature", III, "Egyptian Modernists", *Studies on the Civilization of Islam*, London, 1962, p. 270.

[70] Ğamil Ğabr, *Amīn al-Rayḥānī al-rağul, al-adīb*, p. 25.

[71] See Ch. VI.

became the preacher of a creed superseding all existing ones and excluding none, saying that man via a long chain of individual rebirths will finally lose his individuality and be reunited with God [72].

---

[72] See Ch. VII.

II. THE LIFE OF MĪKHĀ'ĪL NU'AYMAH

Mīkhā'īl Nu'aymah was born in October or November 1889 in Biskintā [1], a mountain village approx. 50 km. N.E. of Beirut. He was the third son of a Greek-Orthodox family of five boys and one girl [2]. The family lived together with the mother's parents in a mud house on the steep slopes of the mountain. They were occupied in all sorts of activities that could bring in money, as the raising of silk worms, agriculture, the holding of small cattle, etc.[3]. The level of existence was low, but in the village the first signs of an increasing income could be observed. Mīkhā'īl's maternal uncles could afford to have a brick house built after they had been engaged in business in Egypt [4]. Others went to the Americas to earn money, and among them was Mīkhā'īl's father. He left shortly after his son Mīkhā'īl had been born but returned six years afterwards with only a little money saved [5].

Mīkhā'īl's mother soon perceived that to achieve success it was necessary to be able to read and write, and therefore she saw to it that her children went to school. However, apart from reading and copying a few Psalms, little could be learned in Biskinta [6]. A change for the better came in 1899, when the Russian "Imperial Orthodox Palestine Society" decided to set up a school in the village [7]. Originally the Society

---

1 *Sab'ūn. Ḥikāyat 'Umr* (Seventy. A Life Story). Autobiography of Mīkhā'īl Nu'aymah. First edition, Beirut, 1959-1960, in three volumes. The footnotes refer to the second edition of volumes one and two, Beirut, 1962 and Beirut, 1964, and to the first edition of volume three. The date of Nu'aymah's birth is given by C. Brockelmann, GALS III, 472, as November 22, 1889. Nu'aymah's own account proves that no record of his birth was kept, and that his parents had forgotten the exact date when he required a birth-certificate to go to Nazareth in 1902 (*Sab'ūn* I, 103-107). Nu'aymah himself believes October 17 to be his birth-day after he had seen that date in a dream when he had returned to Lebanon from America (*Sab'ūn* I, 107). Cf. Ch. V, p. 72f.

2 The senior brothers were Adīb and Haykal (*Sab'ūn* I, 16); Naǧīb was born in 1900 (*Sab'ūn* I, 94) and Nasīb and his sister Ghāliyah were born during Mīkhā'īl's absence in Nazareth (*Sab'ūn* I, 140).

3 *Sab'ūn* I, 15-25.

4 *Sab'ūn* I, 27.

5 *Sab'ūn* I, 15 and 60 f.

6 *Sab'ūn* I, 54 ff.

7 *Sab'ūn* I, 74 f. The "Orthodox Palestine Society", from 1889 "Imperial Palestine Society", was founded in 1882 by the Tsar, the Foreign Ministry and the Procurator of the Synod, after a period of increasing apprehension about the state of affairs of the Orthodox Church in Palestine (Derek Hopwood, *The Russian Presence in Syria and Palestine, 1834-1914*, Oxford, 1969, p. 103 and p. 110). Alarmed by the decreasing number of adherents in Palestine, the Holy Synod of Russia had sent the Archimandrite Porfiri Uspenski to gather information. In 1844 he reported that the local churches were being neglected by the Greek hierarchy; that Arabs were barred from the higher church func-

had been formed by the Holy Synod of the Orthodox Church in Russia to train Arab boys for priesthood. The opposition of the Greek clergy in Palestine however, was so strong that this plan had to be abandonned. The Society then set up a network of schools all over Palestine, Syria and Lebanon with a training school in Nazareth. In doing this they followed the steps of others [8], especially the American Presbyterian schools which, because of their proselytizing force, were a cause of concern for the Orthodox [9], as they had been for the Roman Catholics. The latter, however, had responded to the challenge immediately, whereas the Orthodox schooling program was conceived almost 75 years after the American Presbyterian missionaries had come to Beirut [10].

For Mīkhā'īl this new school in Biskintā was the beginning of an education which would bring him to Nazareth [11] and to Poltava, Ukraine [12]. On account of his excellent grades at the village school he was selected in 1902 to go to the training school of the Society in Nazareth, and in 1906 to attend the Diocesan Seminary in Poltava. It then lay within his reach to occupy a high clerical function, when he would finish the six year course at the Seminary and would study another four years at a theological Academy in Russia [13].

Nu'aymah, however, did not become a priest, and it is not clear if he ever aspired to a position in the Church. In one of his essays he writes that he felt no inclination to become a teacher, nor was attracted by the priesthood. The bar, which would also suit his oratorical gifts, he disliked, he states in the same essay, nevertheless he turned to the study of law because it would afford him an income and leave him

---

tions; and that the Greek hierarchy was lacking in theological eduction; and positions in the church were being bought and sold (Hopwood, 39). The Society then decided to follow the example set by other European powers, supporting a system of Arab schools. This matter had some urgency because more and more Orthodox children were sent to schools which worked under the supervision of English, French and American missionary societies (Hopwood, 137 and 140). The American Presbyterians, especially, attracted children of Orthodox families. In 1895 the Imperial Orthodox Society extented its activities to Syria and Lebanon after the Patriarch of Antioch had called in the Society to bolster his position. In the next ten years the Society set up 77 schools with some 9000 pupils in this area (Hopwood, 150).

8 The first American missionary school in Syria was founded in July, 1824 (A. L. Tibawi, "The American Missionaries". *Middle Eastern Affairs*, No. 3, London, 1963, p. 147). The American University of Beirut celebrated its centenary in 1966.

9 See p. 42 note 7.

10 Concerning the American Missionaries see above p. 5 f.

11 *Sab'ūn* I, 117 ff.

12 *Sab'ūn* I, 171 ff.

13 *Sab'ūn* I, 171 and Mīkhā'īl Nu'aymah, *Ab'ad min Mūskū wa min Washinṭun*, 2nd impression, Beirut, 1961, p. 65 and 70.

time for literary activities [14]. These words, however, date from many years after such a choice could have constituted a dilemma for him. They do not explain why he was so eager to go to Poltava, for as soon as he had heard in Nazareth that every year the best pupil of the fourth year was sent to a Diocesan Seminary in Russia, he himself had decided to be that pupil. To dispell all doubts about his eventual selection he worked hard so as to achieve the highest grades [15]. Since, however, the Diocesan Seminary was the only possibility for him to receive a secondary education at all, it may have been for him nothing more than the next step [16].

If Nu'aymah ever cherished the thought of becoming a priest he must have abandoned it soon after his arrival in Russia. The Archimandrite Uspenski was shocked by the lack of splendour in the churches of Palestine and Syria, when he travelled there in 1842-1844 [17]. Nu'aymah was equally offended by the pomp in the churches in Russia. In the diary he kept in Poltava in 1908 and 1909 he wrote in the entry of April 6th, 1908 : "What is the good of worship when it distracts the heart from its object? In a Christianity that makes you forget the Messias? He likens the church to a theater and the priests to actors : "The sparkling gems on the crown of the Bishop, the candlesticks, the movements of the deacons, the voices of the singers, the smell of the incense, they all divert the attention of the believers" [18].

A definite end to Nu'aymah's training for an ecclesiastical position came during his fourth year in Poltava, when he was expelled from the Seminary for having delivered a seditious speech during a students' strike. The reason for unrest among the students was the abolition of certain privileges they had enjoyed since the 1905 revolution. Nu'aymah's class assumed the leadership of the protest action because the students of the fifth and sixth year were occupied with practical training, and were consequently less inclined to become involved in this kind of worldly affairs. Nu'aymah asserts that he was unaware of it all, and that by chance he entered the room where the strikers convened. When the line of speakers had been exhausted and

---

14 From the essay "al-Muwağğih al-a'ẓam" (The Supreme Director) in Mīkhā'īl Nu'aymah, *al-Nūr wa al-dayǧūr* (Light and Darkness), Beirut, 1963, 3rd impr., p. 133 f.

15 *Sab'ūn* I, 141.

16 In the essay "al-Muwağğih al-a'ẓam" (cf. note 14 above) Nu'aymah mentioned the exact amount he would be able to earn on the basis of each of the diplomas he had received from the various schools he had attented. As a teacher of the lower forms of an elementary school he would earn 20 Franks. The diploma of the Seminary in Nazareth would qualify him to become a headmaster of an elementary school at a salary of 55 Franks. The four-year diploma of Poltava made it possible for him to become a teacher at a Seminary, such as the one in Nazareth, at a salary of over 100 Francs (p. 132 f.). The periods during which the salaries were paid are not mentioned.

17 D. Hopwood, *The Russian Presence in Syria and Palestine, 1843-1914*, Oxford, 1969, p. 36 f.

18 *Sab'ūn* I, 185 f.

a drop in the enthusiasm threatened, he delivered the speech that caused his expulsion. He was excluded from all lessons at the Seminary, but he was not deprived of the right to sit for the fourth class examination one year later than usual. By special ruling, however, he was admitted to the examination in February, 1911 [19].

Of all subjects that were taught at the Seminary, literature was the one most appreciated by Nu'aymah. In Nazareth he had already made his first steps in the field of Russian letters. He had begun with the stories of Chekhov and, too young to enjoy it to the full perhaps, with Dostoevsky's *Crime and Punishment*. In Poltava he extended his acquaintance with the Russian authors, reading *The Demon* by Lermontov, *War and Peace*, *Anna Karenina*, and the ethical writings of Tolstoy, the poetry of Pisemski and of Nadson, novels by Gorky and by Orenburgsky, *The Philosophy of the Russian Literature* by Andreevich, plays by Ostrovsky, stories by Gogol, and so on [20]. Highest among these books ranked with him the ethical works of Tolstoy, about whom he wrote in his diary : "Tolstoy, the searcher for the truth of his Self and of the world around him, attracted me even more than Tolstoy, the author of *War and Peace* and *Anna Karenina*... My guiding light was the same as Tolstoy's : the Gospel. It depressed me, as it did him, that the Church veiled the light of that lamp from the believers with thick curtains of rites and customs [21].

The Russian authors inspired him to write poetry himself and to try his hand on other literary genres. He followed Nikitin's example by keeping a diary [22], and he began to write a play [23]. Hardly anything of it has been kept, except for one poem and his Poltavan diary of which fragments (in Arabic) have been included in the autobiography [24].

According to his own account, Nu'aymah took part in the social life that was open to the students of the Seminary. It included visits to the theater, to the public library (until it was declared out of bounds for the students), and to two dances a year

---

19 *Ab'ad min Mūskū wa min Washinṭun*, p. 84-88; *Sab'ūn* I, 253-255.

20 The names mentioned here all occur in *Sab'ūn* as follows : Chekhov and *Crime and Punishment*, *Sab'ūn* I, 142; Lermontov, *The Demon*, *Sab'ūn* I, 179; Nikitin, *Sab'ūn* I, 179; Pisemsky, *Sab'ūn* I, 183; *War and Peace*, *Sab'ūn* I, 187; Nadson, *Sab'ūn* I, 194; Gorky and Orenburgsky, *Sab'ūn* I, 228; Andreevich, *Sab'ūn* I, 231; Ostrovsky and Gogol, *Sab'ūn* I, 239; Artsybashev, *Sab'ūn* I, 255.

21 *Sab'ūn* I, 269. Literally : The one lamp the light of which I had taken as a guide was the lamp by the light of which Tolstoy was travelling".

22 *Sab'ūn* I, 179.

23 *Sab'ūn* I, 223.

24 *Sab'ūn* I, 179-194. More fragments of the diary have been included in the following pages, but these fragments are no longer dated, chronologically ordered or exactly rendered (*Sab'ūn* I, 194). The last date in the diary is April 21, 1909).

with the pupils of the Diocesan school for girls [25]. The free intercourse between sexes puzzled him at first, but he seems to have become accustomed to it soon. Next to good male friends he had in due time a number of girl-friends, with whom he did not fall in love, as he writes in his autobiography [26]. His relation with Varya, however, was a different affair altogether. She was the married sister of Nu'aymah's friend Ilyusha, and lived quite a distance from the Seminary. Spending his holidays at their farm Nu'aymah discovered that Kutya, the husband, was a moron, and that Varya suffered from this unequal marriage [27]. The autobiography of Nu'aymah informs us that he did not want any relation of love to develop between them, but that, in spite of his resolutions, they became intimate in the end [28]. The liaison was of a short duration, ending with Nu'aymah's departure for Lebanon in 1911, after he had passed his examination [29]. Their plan to remove Kutya as an obstacle to their marriage by sending him to a convent at Mount Athos, failed, because Kutya was not accepted as a monk [30]. The last Nu'aymah heard from Varya was when he arrived in the U.S.A. in the beginning of 1912. She had come to Lebanon after she had succeeded where Kutya had failed in having him accepted by a convent [31].

As regards plans for the future, in Poltava already, after his expulsion from the Seminary, Nu'aymah had decided to seek his admission to the Sorbonne as a student of law. He was inspired to take this step by his friend Mīkhā'īl Iskandar, one year his senior in Nazareth and Poltava, who had broken off his studies in Russia in 1910 to take up law at the Sorbonne [32]. Both counted upon their emigrant brothers in America for financial support. These, however, preferred their new country over Paris, which they judged a dangerous city in moral respects [33]. It so happened that Nu'aymah went to his brothers Adīb and Haykal who lived in Walla Walla, in the State of Washington on the West Coast of America [34].

The main obstacle in the way of Nu'aymah beginning his studies at the University in Seattle, the capital of the State of Washington, was the English language. He solved the problem by attending lessons in a primary, and later in a secondary school during the period that separated him from the new academic year, that is to say

[25] *Sab'ūn* I, 176.
[26] *Sab'ūn* I, 192 f., 233-237.
[27] *Sab'ūn* I, 199 and 213-217.
[28] *Sab'ūn* I, 256 f.
[29] *Sab'ūn* I, 265.
[30] *Sab'ūn* I, 267.
[31] *Sab'ūn* II, 19 f.
[32] *Sab'ūn* I, 264.
[33] *Sab'ūn* I, 280-283.
[34] *Sab'ūn* I, 282 f.

from January until July 1912 [35]. He then entered the University as a student of English Literature and of Law. In the summer of 1916 he took his B.A. degrees in these two subjects [36].

As regards the financial aspects of his studies, Nu'aymah succeeded in making himself independent of his brothers after the outbreak of the World War I. He found a job as a typist for two hours per day at the newly opened Russian consulate in Seattle [37]. These services were rewarded not only with a salary, but, upon Nu'aymah's leaving Seattle for New York, also with three letters of recommendation addressed to other Russian agencies in the U.S.A.[38]. On the strength of these letters Nu'aymah worked as a typist first for the Russian "Mercantile Marine" office in New York [39], and after two months as secretary to the Russian Inspector at the Bethlehem Steel Company, where important Russian Government orders for military equipment had been placed [40]. In this last function Nu'aymah worked until all Russian wartime offices in the U.S.A. were closed after the October revolution.

The most important events during Nu'aymah's stay in Seattle lay outside the field of his studies. During his third year he was introduced to the teachings of theosophy by a Scottish roommate [41]. The idea of the gradual purification of the soul during a series of lives on earth became the core of his beliefs, inspiring him to several of his stories and novels [42]. The aversion of Theosophists to the practice of law [43] may also have been instrumental in Nu'aymah's decision not to seek an occupation in this direction. Freemasonry, to which he was introduced by his brother Adīb, had less attraction for him. After his initiation to the Masonic Lodge of Walla Walla in 1916, he dissociated himself from it once he had arrived in New York, "keeping the kernels and throwing the chaff" [44].

Another significant occurrence during this period was the appearance of *al-Funūn* (The Arts), an Arabic literary magazine published in New York by Nasīb 'Arīḍah, a former schoolmate of Nu'aymah in Nazareth [45]. Nu'aymah greeted this magazine

---

35 *Sab'ūn* II, 15-20.
36 *Sab'ūn* II, 21 f., 59. Facsimile copies of the two B. A. certificates between p. 64 and 65.
37 *Sab'ūn* II, 41.
38 *Sab'ūn* II, 59.
39 *Sab'ūn* II, 67.
40 *Sab'ūn* II, 68.
41 *Sab'ūn* II, 42-48.
42 See Chapter IV.
43 So H. P. Blavatsky, *The Key to Theosophy*, London, 1893[3], p. 38.
44 *Sab'ūn* II, 64.
45 *Al-Funūn* was published in New York from April till December 1913, nine issues appearing in

with great enthusiasm, not only because it re-established his contact with an old friend, but also because he discovered in it a new approach to Arabic Literature [46]. He expressed his feelings in a long article which he sent to Nasīb 'Arīḍah, who published it in the next issue of the magazine [47]. Nu'aymah was so much carried away by *al-Funūn* that, after having obtained his degrees in 1916 [48], he went to New York to edit it jointly with Nasīb 'Arīḍah [49]. Nu'aymah was warmly welcomed by his friend and by the small literary group that convened in the office of the magazine, but for a living he had to look elsewhere [50]. The letters of recommendation he had received proved to be very useful to him at this time.

The closing down of all Russian wartime offices in the U.S.A. meant for Nu'aymah that he was no longer employed by an allied power, and that he would be drafted into the United States army [51]. Nu'aymah explains in his autobiography how he became involved in the war, even though he was not an American subject. The U.S. government, on entering the war, had issued a ruling ordering all young men between the ages of 21 and 30 to register their names at the nearest conscription center. Not everybody obeyed, but Nu'aymah did, because, "being bound to the law is part of my character" [52]. In another place he writes : "I had no other excuse to remain free from compulsory service in the American army than being a Turkish subject.

all; from June 1916-May 1917, 12 issues appeared; from August 1917-November 1917, four issues; from April 1918-August 1918, four issues, a total of 29 issues. This at least is the number of issues available at the New York Public Library, of which a photostat copy is kept in the Cambridge University Library. Number I, 7 (October, 1913) is missing and therefore the set is not as complete as Nadeem Naimy, *Mikhail Naimy*, (Ph. D. Thesis, Cambridge; Beirut, 1967, p. 112-117), says it is, or this number was never published. *Al-Funūn* was a purely literary magazine, and as such preceded *Apollo*, which was published in Egypt from September 1932 until 1936. Muḥammad Mandūr's assertion that *Apollo* was the first literary magazine in Arabic is therefore not correct (M. Mandūr, *Muḥāḍarāt fī al-shi'r al-miṣrī ba'da Shawqī* (Lectures on Arabic poetry after Shawqī), Vol. I, Cairo, 1955, p. 22.

46 *Sab'ūn* II, 28-29.

47 The title of this article is "Faǧr al-amal ba'da layl al-yā's", "The Dawn of Hope after the Night of Despair", *al-Funūn* I, 4 (July 1913), p. 50-70.

48 *Sab'ūn* II, 59.

49 *Sab'ūn* II, 65-67. Nasīb 'Arīḍah, born in Homs about 1889, died in New York, 1946. His contribution to Arabic literature consisted mainly in his efforts to create a literary magazine. He was publisher and editor of *al-Funūn*, and afterwards he was editor of *al-Sā'iḥ*, an Arabic newspaper in New York, which would eventually open its columns to literary work after *al-Funūn* had to be discontinued for financial reasons.

50 *Sab'ūn* II, 66 f. On this occasion Nu'aymah met Khalīl Ǧibrān for the first time. Concerning Ǧibrān see note 66 below.

51 *Sab'ūn* II, 72-125. These pages contain Nu'aymah's impressions of life in the army and on the battle-field.

52 *Sab'ūn* II, 73.

I felt myself above seeking recourse to such an excuse" [53]. Nasīb 'Arīḍah, however, in a farewell article in *al-Funūn*, quotes Nu'aymah as having often said that "he did not have the right to inhale this air and to enjoy the light of the sun and the pleasure of life as long as thousands of others were sacrificing the good things of life for freedom, and", Nasīb 'Arīḍah continues, "how often he was astonished about us — Syrian youth — sitting down in the shade doing no harm nor good to mankind, whereas the youngsters of other nations threw themselves into the presses of the peoples so that a few drops of blood would remain of their bodies to moisten the field of humanity" [54].

In October, 1918, Nu'aymah went to France, where he participated in the last battles of the war [55]. Waiting for his transport back to the U.S.A. he was one of the American soldiers who where allowed to study at a French university as a token of friendship between France and the U.S.A. During four months he attended lectures at the University of Rennes on French History, Literature and Art, and on the French Constitution. He also followed a course in French, especially designed for American soldiers [56].

The end of the war required new decisions. Nu'aymah had finished his studies in the U.S.A., and the main obstacle blocking his way home had been removed. The war was over and Turkish rule, hated and feared in Syria and Lebanon, had come to an end. The future status of the area was still debated by the four great powers, but everything pointed in the direction of a French mandate. The final decision was reached on April 25, 1920 at the Peace Conference in San Remo, where France was recognized as the mandatory power in Syria and Lebanon [57]. It is unlikely, however, that these new developments had any influence on Nu'aymah's decision to return to the United States. In his autobiography Nu'aymah writes that he decided to return to New York, although he did not know how to earn a living there, and although *al-Funūn* had ceased to appear, because he was determined to pursue his efforts to modernize Arabic literature [58]. Whatever the truth of this statement, the fact is that he had found in New York a circle of friends who shared the same ideas about Arabic literature, and who must have had a sort of in-crowd attraction for Nu'aymah.

---

[53] Nu'aymah, *Ab'ad min Mūskū wa min Washinṭun* (Far from Moscow and Washington), p. 102.

[54] *al-Funūn* III, 8 (August, 1918), p. 616 f.

[55] *Sab'ūn* II, 109-119.

[56] *Sab'ūn* II, 126-134.

[57] For more information on this subject see : G. Antonius, *The Arab Awakening*, London, repr. 1955[3], p. 276 ff. and J. Nantet, *Histoire du Liban*, Paris, 1963, p. 246.

[58] *Sab'ūn* II, 134.

In New York Nu'aymah found a job as travelling salesman for three Lebanese brothers who imported ladies pyjamas and embroidered babyclothes from the Philipines [59]. He worked with them until after five years, at the end of 1925, the firm went bankrupt [60]. Then followed some irregular jobs. One man employed him to sell plots of land to the readers of an Arabic newspaper "*al-Sā'iḥ*" (The Traveller) [61], to which Nu'aymah had frequently contributed. After that the same man hired him for an exhibition of Oriental products in New York. This job brought Nu'aymah into contact with an Indian who introduced him to Vivekananda's *Raja Yoga* and to the *Bhagavad Gita* [62]. A fortnight's selling of the *Encyclopedia Britannica* to well-to-do Arabs in New York earned him 750 dollar [63]. Finally he was employed by a Syrian merchant who charged him with the purchase and selling of Philipine embroideries [64]. With this firm Nu'aymah stayed another five years until he left the United States, on April 19, 1932.

Notwithstanding these commercial occupations, Nu'aymah was able to spend some time on literature. He wrote essays, poetry, short stories, a play, and the first part of a novel in these years. Most of these writings were contributions to *al-Funūn* and to the newspaper *al-Sā'iḥ*. The play was published in book form, and a number of the essays were collected in one volume when Nu'aymah was still in America [65]. The stories, the poetry and a large number of essays remained scattered in various periodicals until they were republished in several volumes long after his return to Lebanon.

To Nu'aymah's literary activities must also be added the hours he spent together with Khalīl Ǧibrān, Nasīb 'Arīḍah, Rashīd Ayyūb, 'Abdel-Masīḥ Ḥaddād, William Kātsiflīs, Nadrah Ḥaddād, Wādī' Bāḥūṭ, Ilyās 'Aṭā Allāh and Īlīyā Abū Māḍī [66].

---

59 *Sab'ūn* II, 141 f.

60 *Sab'ūn* II, 233 f.

61 *Al-Sā'iḥ* was an Arabic newspaper founded by 'Abd al-Masīḥ Ḥaddād. In a few years this paper developed from a bi-weekly into a daily. In 1957 'Abd al-Masīḥ Ḥaddād sold the paper to Dr. Rāǧī al-Ẓāhir ('Īsā al-Nā'ūrī, *Adab al-mahǧar*, p. 21, Cairo, 1959).

62 *Sab'ūn* II, 242.

63 *Sab'ūn* II, 244.

64 *Sab'ūn* II, 257.

65 The play, the title of which is *al-Ābā' wa al-banūn* (Fathers and Sons), was serialized in *al-Funūn*, Vol. II, 7 (December 1916), II, 8 (January, 1917), II, 9 (February, 1917), II, 10 (March, 1917) and II, 11 (April, 1917). It was first published by Dār al-Funūn, New York, 1917. *Al-Ghirbāl* is a volume of essays on Arabic literature. It was first published in Cairo, 1923.

66 Ǧibrān Khalīl Ǧibrān (or Kahlil Gibran as he styled his name in English) was born in Lebanon 1883 and died in New York, April, 10, 1931. He is perhaps more famous outside the Arab world than in it, on account of his book *The Prophet* (1st ed. 1923). Nu'aymah was one of the first to write a biography of Ǧibrān after the latter's death (Cf. Chapter V). Of the others Īlīyā Abū Māḍī and

Together they created *al-Rābiṭah al-qalamiyyah* (The Pen Bond) on April 20th, 1920, with Ǧibrān as chairman and Nu'aymah as secretary [67]. Nasīb 'Arīḍah had originally proposed to form a trade-union with the aim to protecting the rights of the authors against the owners of newpapers [68]. *Arrabitah*, as it was abbreviated in English, had a different and more ambitious program. Its membership was divided into three categories : Workers, Sympathizers and Correspondents. The category of the workers, or active members, was restricted to the ten persons mentioned above [69]. They agreed on the following tasks : to publish the works of the members and of other writers *Arrabitah* might consider worth publishing, as well as to encourage the translation of the masterpieces of world literature into Arabic; to foster new talent by offering prizes for the best in poetry and prose [70]. Lack of funds made it impossible to implement this program. The only publication *Arrabitah* ever undertook was the annual *Maǧmū'ah* (Collection) for the year 1921. The Arab colony in the U.S.A., however, was not ripe for such a publication, and for the Arabs elsewhere it was too expensive. The result was a financial débacle which discouraged the members from making another attempt [71]. Meanwhile they had found in the annual special issue of *al-Sā'iḥ* (The Traveller) a good, though more modest, replacement for the *Maǧmū'ah*. As an addition to the newspaper the special issue was distributed freely

---

Rashīd Ayyūb achieved some fame. Īlīyā Abū Māḍī (born 1890 in Lebanon, died in 1957, in New York) composed five volumes of poetry : *Tidhkār al-māḍī* (A Token of the Past or A Token of Abū Māḍī); *Dīwān Īlīyā Abū Māḍī*; *al-Ǧadāwil* (The brooks); *al-Khamā'il* (The Woods); *Tibr wa turāb* (Golddust and dust). Rashīd Ayyūb (born 1872 in Biskintā, Lebanon, died December 27, 1941, in Brooklyn). He published three volumes of poetry : *Al-Ayyūbiyyāt* (Poems of Ayyūb); *Aghānī al-Darwīsh* (Songs of the derwish); *Hiya al-dunyā* (This is the world).

67 *Sab'ūn* II, 163-175.

68 *Sab'ūn* II, 54.

69 *Sab'ūn* II, 163.

70 Mīkhā'īl Nu'aymah, *Ǧibrān Khalīl Ǧibrān ḥayātuhu, mawtuhu, adabuhu, fannuhu.* (His Life, his Death, his Literature, his Art), Beirut, 4th impr., 1960, p. 159. Mikhail Naimy, *Kahlil Gibran. His Life and Work* (English text), Beirut, second impr., 1965, p. 155. At least one thesis has been written on *Arrabitah* : Nādirah Sarrāǧ, *Shu'arā al-rābiṭah al-qalamiyyah*, Cairo, 1957. Other books in Arabic discussing *al-Rābiṭah* are : 'Īsā al-Nā'ūrī, *Adab al-mahǧar*, Cairo, 1959, 'Abd al-Karīm al-Ashtar, *al-Nathr al-mahǧarī* (Prose by Emigrants), 2 vols. Cairo, 1961, and Wadī' Rashīd al-Khūrī, *Ẓuhūr wa taṭawwur al-adab al-'arabī fī al-mahǧar al-amīrkī*, Beirut, 1969. Wadī' Rashīd al-Khūrī reveals that the name *al-Rābiṭah al-qalamiyyah* occurred already in the first and third issues of the second year of *al-Funūn*, in June and August 1916, and that it consisted of five members only : William Kātsiflīs, 'Abd al-Masīḥ Ḥaddād, Ǧibrān Khalīl Ǧibrān, Rashīd Ayyūb and Naṣīb 'Arīḍah (p. 28). Of the other literary groups that were formed, the *Dīwān*-group in Egypt has been mentioned (see above p. 10). The Apollo-group in Egypt was named after its magazine *Apollo*, which was published from September 1932 until 1935. The Syrian *al-Rābiṭah al-adabiyyah* was formed in 1921. The French mandatory power put an end to its activities in 1923. In St. Paolo in Brasil *al-'Uṣbah al-andalusiyyah* was founded in 1933. They published the magazine *al-'Uṣbah* ('Īsā al-Nā'ūrī, *Adab al-mahǧar*, p. 24-28).

71 *Sab'ūn* II, 165.

to the subscribers which meant that this annual could be issued as long as the newspaper prospered [72]. Unfortunately, in 1931, as a result of the general financial situation in the U.S.A., the number of advertisers dropped below the number which was required to publish the special issue of *al-Sā'iḥ* [73].

The fame of *Arrabitah* spread quickly among the Arabs in America, and they became known in the Arab countries as well. One of the reasons for this may be found in their rule requiring contributors to sign articles in magazines and newspapers with their names and the words "Worker of *Arrabitah*" [74]. The movement seems to have petered out after the death of Ǧibrān, April 10, 1931, and the departure from the U.S.A. of Nu'aymah one year later.

Nu'aymah remained his whole life a bachelor, although he was not indifferent towards the fair sex during a certain period of his life. Some time before he left the United States he seems to have decided not to marry, and to sublimate his sexual desire into spiritual love. In the third part of his autobiography, which describes his life in Lebanon from 1931 onwards, he writes "I still looked at a woman from the point of view of a man, but with the looks of somebody who believes that a woman and a man cannot perfect each other's humanity by the marriage of their bodies but by that of their spirits; I believed that physical marriage impedes the spiritual wedding. The thought of marriage, therefore, I banned out of my life [75]. It is possible to argue that the ideas of Nu'aymah were not uncommon at that time, and that many Arab authors remained unmarried. This does not explain, however, why Nu'aymah, as it were, in principle converted to bachelordom. His relations with Bella, and especially with Neonia, or Njonja, during his stay in the United States are very probably at the basis of his decision.

In 1919, Nu'aymah became acquainted with Bella, his landlady, who like Varya in Russia, was unhappily married. Her husband Harry, is described by Nu'aymah as a drunkard and a *primitif*. She had been wedded to this man at the age of sixteen by her guardian on the instigation of Harry's mother [76]. Nu'aymah's relation with Bella lasted five years. The end came when Harry, after a long period of abstinence, slid back into his old habit. Nu'aymah left the house being under the impression that it was his liaison with Bella that had caused Harry's relapse.

---

[72] Nu'aymah, *Ǧibrān Khalīl Ǧibrān* (Arabic ed.), p. 161, English ed. p. 157. Already in 1915 Nasīb 'Arīḍah had planned to issue a special number of *al-Sā'iḥ*. The letter dated November 19, 1915, referring to it has been included in *Sab'ūn* II, 51 ff.

[73] *Sab'ūn* II, 292.

[74] Nu'aymah, *Ǧibrān Khalīl Ǧibrān* (Arabic version), p. 161, English version, p. 157.

[75] *Sab'ūn* III, 99.

[76] *Sab'ūn* II, 151 ff. The names are fictitious, says Nu'aymah.

The relation with Njonja was completely different. She was a Polish lady, about 25 years of age and a "Lionness", as Nu'aymah describes her [77]. He became acquainted with her through a friend of his in the summer of 1929 [78]. Most of the time they met she was in the company of an Italian painter and of a musician. Their constant presence puzzled Nu'aymah, but it did not occur to him to ask her about her relations with these men : "She might consider it jealousy on my part or doubt of her loyalty towards me, or see it as an encroachment on her private life' [79]. The latitude he left her had no correspondence in his own life. According to his own accounts he could have had three mistresses next to Njonja but "I did not want any connection with a girl, however understanding, tempting and beautiful she might be, to defile the love between me and Njonja" [80]. He must, therefore, have been profoundly shocked when Njonja told him she was married to the painter, the more so because she always had used her maiden name [81]. He must have understood at the same time that in all probability he was not the only friend she had next to her husband. This time Nu'aymah's mistress was not an unhappy human being in need of a conforting hand, but somebody with energy to spare. In spite of all this Nu'aymah could not break off his relations with her [82]. Even her unconcern for his thoughts about life and death, good and evil, and the purpose of existence failed to diminish his love for her [83]. It is possible that this relationship with Njonja was responsible for his conception of a rift between physical and spiritual love. What happened after she had revealed to him that she was married is not described by Nu'aymah, except that they met again. He writes in his autobiography that they had decided to break off the relation, and that they failed. Soon afterwards he left America for Lebanon to live by his pen and to purify his soul of the sexual urge [84].

Nu'aymah was able to return to Lebanon in April, 1932, because all the reasons that had encouraged him to stay in America had been removed. The war had ended; Ğibrān's death had had a paralyzing effect on *Arrabitah*, as must have had the financial crisis in America. Thus it seemed that *Arrabitah's* mission had ended [85], and Nu'aymah's younger brother Nasīb was no longer in need of financial support. This brother

[77] *Sab'ūn* II, 289.
[78] *Sab'ūn* II, 285.
[79] *Sab'ūn* II, 288.
[80] *Sab'ūn* II, 288.
[81] *Sab'ūn* II, 285 and 308.
[82] *Sab'ūn* II, 319.
[83] *Sab'ūn* II, 289 f.
[84] *Sab'ūn* II, 320.
[85] Nu'aymah writes that *Arrabitah* had fulfilled its mission after it had brought the combat in the interest of the Arabic language (*kifāḥ fī sabīl al-kalimah*) to where it should be — the Arab region (*Sab'ūn* II, 320).

had depended upon Nu'aymah, who financed his agricultural studies in France. In 1931 Nasīb had taken his degree in agricultural engineering at the University of Nancy and had returned to Lebanon [86]. There it was very soon discovered that he had contracted tuberculosis, which incapacitated him and caused his death on May 15, 1933 [87]. For Nu'aymah it meant that he again, this time in Lebanon, had to share in the support of the family. As far as time and his physical powers permitted, he worked on the land. Much of his energy, however, went into unsalaried social activities, or into contemplation and writing. At various meetings he spoke about the beauties of Lebanon, the message of the East, the decay of the Western world, and other subjects [88].

In his autobiography Nu'aymah complains that without remuneration he had to deliver speeches, do all kind of administrative work, and act as a secretary for his fellow-villagers who were unable to write [89]. On the other hand he had to see his publications through the press and bear all the costs himself [90]. Only in 1945, was he able to conclude his first contract with a publisher who would pay him a fixed percentage of the retail price of the book on the date of publication [91]. During the war he delivered monthly talks on the radio, which were extremely well paid. His contributions to periodicals and his speeches before clubs also brought in some money. From this time onwards he has been able to live on his own earnings while devoting his life to writing [92]. Only once has he left the Arab world, for a visit to the Soviet Union, in 1956, at the invitation of the Writers' Union in Moscow [93]. The remainder of his time he has passed in Biskintā, in nearby Shakhrub, and, during the winters mostly in Beirut.

---

86 *Sab'ūn* II, 318. After his return to Lebanon, Nasīb taught French language at the "National University" of Aley, Lebanon.

87 *Sab'ūn* III, 23 and 85 ff.

88 *Sab'ūn* III, 48., 124 f., cf. the speech he delivered at the "welcome home" party, p. 41-47.

89 *Sab'ūn* III, 124 f.

90 *Sab'ūn* III, 58 f.

91 *Sab'ūn* III, 161 f.

92 *Sab'ūn* III, 160 ff.

93 *Sab'ūn* III, 222 and *Ab'ad min Mūskū wa min Washinṭun*, 2nd impression, Beirut, 1961.

III. THE LITERARY WORK : POETRY

Like others of his generation Nuʿaymah had a universal concept of his penmanship. He claimed he had a message to convey, not only to the people of his kin, but to the world at large, and therefore he sometimes wrote in English or translated his original Arabic works into that language. The vehicle for this message could be anything, from a poem to a play, and from an essay or speech to a short story or novel.

During his stay in Russia, 1906-1911, Nuʿaymah began to write poetry in Russian [1], and he kept a Russian diary [2]. Some two years after his arrival in America, early in 1914, he contributed the first literary essay to the Arabic magazine *al-Funūn* [3], in New York. From then onwards he was a regular contributor to the magazine. Besides essays he wrote Arabic and English poetry, most of which appeared during his years in America [4]. His play *al-Ābāʾ wa al-banūn* (Fathers and Sons) was published in New York, in 1917 [5] and in the same year he began to work on a novel *Mudhakkarāt al-Arqash* (The Memoirs of Pitted Face) which was serialized in *al-Funūn* [6] so far as it went. After four parts Nuʿaymah, who had meanwhile been drafted into the U.S.A. army, discontinued the serial. He resumed his work on the novel in 1948, publishing it the same year. The first short story, "Sanatuhā al-ğadīdah" (Her New Year), dates from 1914. [7]

After almost sixty years of active writing Nuʿaymah's bibliography includes one volume of poems, four volumes of short stories, one biography, a three-volume autobiography, three plays, two of which are simple dialogues for two persons, one volume of aphorisms, four novels, ten volumes of essays, one travelogue, one volume of press

---

1 *Sabʿūn* I, p. 180 footnote 1 relates the first trial. Other poems in Russian are mentioned on page 230, 240 and 257. On p. 257 the poem "The Frozen River" is mentioned, which was translated by the poet into Arabic (cf. *Sabʿūn* II, p. 70) and published in the Arabic magazine *al-Funūn*, second volume, number 9 (February, 1917), p. 732-735, and, shortened by four lines, included in *Hams al-ğufūn*, Beirut, 1962[4], p. 10-13.

2 *Sabʿūn* I, 179.

3 *Sabʿūn* II, 28-29.

4 The poems referred to are those of *Hams al-ğufūn*, first edition, Beirut, 1945. All quotations are from the fourth edition, Beirut, 1962.

5 *Sabʿūn* II, 77.

6 *Sabʿūn* II, 75 f. and III, 210 f.

7 "Sanatuhā al-ğadīdah" (Her New Year), published in *Kān mā kān* (Once upon a Time), p. 39-51 of the 6th impression, Beirut, 1963.

interviews, and what may be called a book of prayers, completed on August 4, 1972, a total of 30 volumes of some 6000 pages [8].

A large part of his writings is devoted to spiritual matters. Most of the essays are really sermons based on the doctrine of metempsychosis and of the ultimate union of the human soul with its divine origin. The urge to convey this creed has resulted a.o. in four novels, three of which may be characterized as variations on Bunyan's *Pilgrim's Progress* [9]. These novels will be dealt with in the next chapter, together with the short stories. The biography of Ǧibrān and Nuʿaymah's autobiography will form the subject-matter of chapter five. Among his other writings deserving special treatment are the literary essays published, for the most part, in *al-Ghirbāl* [10] (The Sieve). The more recent collection *Fī al-ghirbāl al-ǧadīd* (In the New Sieve) consists in the main of profiles of literary men from the Arab East, from Russia and from the West, including writers like Puschkin and Gorky and like Nietzsche and Emerson. The collection comprises also a few reviews of work by Arab authors and poets [11]. To these essays the sixth chapter will be devoted. The seventh and last chapter brings the essays in which Nuʿaymah expounded his beliefs with regard to the human destiny.

Nuʿaymah's one volume of poetry, *Hams al-ǧufūn* (Eyelids' Whisper) [12], contains, besides 30 original poems, 14 Arabic prose renderings of poems he composed in the English language. The earliest of these poems dates from 1917, and the last from 1928. The prose translations are dated from 1925 through 1930, but it is not clear whether these dates refer to the original composition or to the prose translation [13].

The uncommon form of Nuʿaymah's poetry jumps to the eye of everybody who

---

[8] For full details see Bibliography. Most of Nuʿaymah's writings are subject to discussion in this and the following chapters. The two plays *Ayyūb* and *Yā Ibn Ādām!* (O, Son of Man), the volume of aphorisms *Karam ʿalā darb* (A Vineyard by the Road) and the book of prayers *Naǧwā al-ghurūb* (Confidential whispers at sunset) have not been made use of for quotation.

[9] *Liqāʾ* (Encounter). First edition, Beirut, 1948. An English translation of it, together with 12 other stories entitled *Till we meet...*, was published in Bangalore, 1957. *Mudhakkarāt al-Arqash* (Memoirs of Pitted Face). First edition Beirut, 1949. Translated by the author into English and published with the title *Memoirs of a Vagrant Soul*, New York, 1952 (Information derived from Nadeem N. Naimy, *Mikhail Naimy. An Introduction*, Beirut, 1967, p. 163, note 3). *The Book of Mirdad*, Nuʿaymah's third novel, was originally written in English, Beirut, 1948. An Arabic translation entitled *Kitāb Mirdād* was published in Beirut, 1952. A Dutch translation appeared in Haarlem, Rosicrucian Society, 1960. The last novel is *al-Yawm al-akhīr* (The Last Day), Beirut, 1963.

[10] *Al-Ghirbāl*, First impression, Cairo, 1923.

[11] Mīkhāʾīl Nuʿaymah, *al-Maǧmūʿah al-kāmilah* (The Complete Collection), Vol. 7, Beirut, 1973, p. 369-604.

[12] First impression, Beirut, 1945.

[13] The dates are culled from the fourth edition of *Hams al-ǧufūn*, Beirut, 1962.

has ever opened a volume of traditional Arabic poetry. The typical twin monolithic columns of hemistichs are almost completely absent. Instead Nu'aymah used for many of his poems the well-known European one-column type with lines of varying length, a form, which, though not entirely unknown in Arabic poetry, especially in popular poetry, is relatively rare. Nu'aymah, moreover, divided the column into stanzas which is a technique known to the folk song, but hardly ever used in classical poetry.

Nu'aymah has achieved variety in stanzaic forms greater than the number of his poems would seem to warrant. Next to clearcut stanzas, we find stanzas which are not so easily defined. The poem "Ṣadā al-ağrās" [14] (The Voice of the Church-bells) has the rhyme-scheme a a x a, b b x b etc. suggesting a four-line stanza, but it has been typographically divided into stanzas of up to 16 lines. A refrain, spelling out the sound of the church-bell, is sometimes used and sometimes not, making the stanzaic division even more uncertain.

External appearance seems to have determined the division into stanzas of the poem "Ibtihālāt" [5] (Supplications). The twelfth and thirteenth stanza of this poem closely belong together, the twelfth ending with the protasis of a conditional clause, the apodosis of which is contained in the first lines of the thirteenth [16]. On the other hand the metrical system of Nu'aymah's poetry is traditional. In none of his poems has he seriously departed from the usual Arabic metres, but he does allow himself considerable freedom as regards the length of his lines [17]. The longest lines occur in "Bayna 'l-ğamāğim" [18] (Between the Skulls), with 24 syllables per line

[14] *Hams al-ğufūn*, p. 40-45.

[15] *Hams al-ğufūn*, 35-39.

[16] The last two lines of the twelfth stanza of this poem consisting of 20 stanzas are

3. *wa idhā mā qāma ghayrī yadda'ī*
4. *yā ilāhī 'l-haqqa fī buṭlin wa ghayyī*

The thirteenth stanza begins with these lines :

1. *fal-yakun sayfan lisānī ḥadduhū*
2. *fī sabīli 'l-ḥaqqi māḍin lā yahāb*

translated :

3. When somebody comes forth claiming,
4. O God, that the truth is in falsehood and error,
1. let my tongue be a sword with an edge
2. pursuing the road of the truth without fear.

[17] "Aṭ-Ṭuma'nīnah" (Tranquility) (p. 73-74), a dimeter *khafīf* has been used, provided we accept the division into two hemistichs per line as genuine. Other shortenings or apocopations occur in "Min sifri 'z-zamān" (From the Book of Time), p. 26-27, "Ibtihālāt" (Supplications), p. 35-39, "Ṣadā 'l-ağrās" (The Voice of the Churchbells), p. 40-45, "Awrāqu 'l-kharīf" (Autumm Leaves), p. 47-49, "at-Tā'ih" (The Wanderer), p. 52-54, "Unshūdah (Song), p. 65-67, "Tarnīmatu 'r-riyāḥ" (The Hymn of the Winds), p. 87-92.

[18] *Hams al-ğufūn*, p. 99-101.

divided over six feet. The shortest lines count not more than three syllables, but they stand between lines of greater length. A remarkable poem is "Unshūdah" [19] (Song) with its ten syllables per line divided over two hemistichs. It is possible to consider the metre as an apocopated *rağaz* : ⏓ – ⏑ – / – or as a *Shahīn ghazālī* : – – ⏑ – – as signalled by Freytag [20].

The typographical production of Nu'aymah's poems is partly modern, partly traditional, and some poems give occasion to think of a mixed type. Only six of the 30 poems have been printed in the traditional two columns. Another six poems can be considered as representing horizontal mergers of the two columns into one [21]. Instead of being separated by a blank space, the two hemistichs have been printed in one continuous line. The remaining 18 poems have been printed in one column, and seemingly do not consist of half-verses. The idea of the hemistich, however, is not completely absent, as is revealed by a few peculiarities in these poems. Scansion shows irregularities in the metre which can be explained only with reference to the traditional hemistich.

In some of the poems certain lines end with elements which, metrically speaking, belong to the following line. Traditional Arabic poetry allowed such treatment of the two hemistichs of one line of verse only. The equilibrium between the two halves was then restored by stretching the last word of the first hemistich into the second half-verse. When the hemistichs are written one beneath the other a different solution must be sought, as Arabic words are commonly not broken up. One alternative is the division of the metre and this is what Nu'aymah did [22].

---

19 *Hams al-ğufūn*, p. 65-67.

20 G. W. Freytag, *Darstellung der arabischen Verskunst*, Bonn, 1830, p. 74 and especially p. 461 f.

21 The merged poems are : "An-nahru 'l-mutağammid" (The Frozen River), p. 10-13, "Akhī" (My Brother), p. 14-15, "Man anti yā nafsi" (Who are you, my soul?), p. 16-21, "aṭ-Ṭarīq" (The Road), p. 46, "al-'Irāk" (The Struggle), p. 96, "Bayna 'l-ğamāğim" (Between the Skulls), p. 99-101.

22 This peculiar treatment of the metre can be found in "Ḥablu 't-tamannī" (The Rope of Wishing), p. 23, lines one and two from the top :

natamannā wa mā 't-tamannī siwā mihmāzi
dahrin yuḥaththunā li 'l-masīrī

The last two syllables of the first line belong metrically to the second line. Other instances of this metrical division are to be found in the third and fourth lines from the top on the same page, and in lines one and two from the top on p. 25; in "Law tudriku 'l-ashwāq" (If Thorns Could Understand), on p. 31 lines three and two from the bottom, and on p. 32 lines one and two from top, in "Ṣadā 'l-ağrās" (The Sound of the Church-bells), p. 42, lines 8 and 9 from the top, lines 3 and 2 from the bottom. On p. 43 line 3 from the top contains a complete foot which metrically belongs to the following line. The same phenomenon can be observed in the above mentioned lines of p. 31. The metrical jump which occurs seven times in total in "Ṣadā 'l-ağrās" is found also in "Afāqa 'l-qalb" (The Heart Awoke), p. 55-63 and in "Ilā M.D.B." (To M.D.B.), p. 102-107.

A second reminiscence of the two hemistichs in Nu'aymah's one-column poems is enjambment, which is more frequent and more outspoken between lines which could be regarded as hemistichs than elsewhere [23]. On the other hand there are indications that the hemistich has grown out into a complete line of verse in Nu'aymah's poetry. The new arrangement of the poem in one column as well as the adoption of new rhyme schemes have contributed to the emancipation of the hemistich.

In traditional Arabic poetry the second hemistichs of one poem end in the same rhyme, whereas the first hemistichs normally do not rhyme. This so-called monorhyme, in combination with the two-column notation, has been applied by Nu'aymah to three of his poems only [25]. In three others, written in one column, every second line ends in the same rhyme, thus marking the transition from the traditional two columns to the modern form [26]. The majority of his poems have multiple rhyme-schemes, contrasting on the one hand with the traditional poetry, and on the other hand with the modern rhymeless forms of Ğibrān and of Amīn al-Rayḥānī. In a poem such as "Min sifri 'z-zamān" [27] (From the Book of Time) the ryhme-scheme a b b a c c c d d a has been used, which is incompatible with poetry in hemistichia.

The first of the two stanzas of this poem runs as follows :

Rūḥī! Fa-kam shabbat wa-shābat sanīn
min qabli an bānat ḥawāshīkī
wa'l-yawma kaffu 'd-dahri taṭwīkī
'annā, wa man yadrī matā tunsharīn
rūḥī wa-khallīnā
bi 'l-arḍi lāhīnā
nar'ā amānīnā
fī marğī awhāmī
mā bayna ayyāmin wa a'wāmī
ta'tī wa tamḍī wahya sirrun dafīn

[23] E.g. "Ḥablu 't-tamannī" (The Rope of Wishing), p. 22, lines 5 and 6 from the top, p. 23, lines 1 and 2, 3 and 4, p. 25 lines 3 and 4, p. 27 lines 3 and 4.

[24] Footnote elided.

[25] The poems are : "aṭ-Ṭuma'nīnah" (Tranquility), p. 73-74, "al-Hamm" (Anxiety), p. 93, "Yā baḥr" (O Sea), p. 97-98.

[26] "Takhdīru afkār" (Thoughts' Drugging), p. 50-51, "Lammā ra'aytu 'n-nāsu" (After I had Seen Mankind), p. 71-72, "Ilā dūdah" (To a Worm), p. 83-86. A hydrib form is "at-Tā'ih" (The Wanderer), written in two columns with every second line ending with the same rhyme. The uneven lines of this poem do not rhyme.

[27] *Hams al-ğufūn*, p. 26 f. The quoted lines are from p. 26.

"Go forth! How many years were young and grew old
before your train appeared.
Today, the hand of time folds you
away from us. Who knows when you'll be recalled to life again.
Go forth and leave us alone
on the earth, trifling
tending our wishes
in the meadows of our fantasies.
What between days and years
comes and goes is a hidden secret"

The language of Nuʿaymah's poetry does not offer great difficulties. The vocabulary is of the commonest without archaic words or far-fetched idioms [28]. The sentences, generally speaking, are short, as they should be in Arabic poetry, but sometimes whole clusters of sentences do occur.

The first of the five stanzas of "Akhī" [29] (My brother) offers a good example of such a cluster :

Akhī, in ḍağğa baʿda 'l-ḥarbi gharbiyyun bi-aʿmālih
wa qaddasa dhikra man mātū wa ʿaẓẓama baṭsha abṭālih
fa-lā tahzağ li-man sādū, wa lā tashmat bi-man dānā
bali 'rkaʿ ṣāmitan mithlī bi-qalbin khāshiʿin dāmī
li-nabkī ḥaẓẓa mawtānā

"Brother, if after the war the Westerner boasts of his deeds,
hallowing the memory of those who died, and
magnifying the gallantry of his heroes,
do not laud those who gained the upper hand, nor blame those who lost,
but bend the knee like me in silence with a submissive bleeding heart
to weep over the fate of our dead".

This stanza consists of a single conditional sentence, with a protasis stretching over three clauses and an apodosis of four clauses, the last of which is subordinate to the preceding clause.

---

[28] It is exactly this quality which led Dr. Muḥammad Mandūr in *Fī al-mīzān al-ğadīd* (In the New Balance, Cairo (1944)[2], p. 50-64), to speak of "whispered poetry" (*shiʿr mahmūs*). It is noteworthy that Dr. Mandur applies this term to the poem "Akhī", which might be considered the least whispered of Nuʿaymah's poems. See p. 45 f.

[29] *Hams al-ğufūn*, p. 14-15. A translation of this poem into English has been included in *Modern Arabic Poetry*, edited by A. J. Arberry, Cambridge, 1967, p. 65 f.

Another instance of such a composite clause occurs in "Ilā M.D.B." [30] (To M.D.B.). The first stanza of this poem which consists of ten five-line stanzas is as follows :

Anā 's-sirru 'llādhī 'statarā
bi-rūḥiki mundhu mā khaṭarā
bi-bāli 'l-kā'ini 'l-a'lā
khayālu 'l-'ālami 'l-adnā
fa-ṣawwara min tharan basharā

"I am the secret hidden
in your soul since there came
to the mind of the Supreme Being
the spectre of the lower world
and He formed man from mud"

To be remarked in both examples is the low frequency of adjectives, which, moreover, are functional because of their contrastive force. In "My Brother" the "submissive, bleeding heart" contrasts with the verbs "boasts, hallows, and magnifies" and in "To M.D.B." the rhyming adjectives *a'lā* and *adnā* ("Most high" and "Nearest", "Basest", here translated as "Supreme" and "lower") are each other's opposites.

Another characteristic of Nu'aymah's poetical style can be observed in "My Brother" rather than in "To M.D.B.". The three clauses of the protasis enumerate the verbal reactions of the Western soldier on the war. Such kind of enumeration can be found in many of Nu'aymah's poems, and on that account it is permissible to qualify it as belonging to his style. Now, it appears that enumeration has never been a foreign element in Arabic poetry. Its germ may be found in the Arab ideal of the line of verse as a self-contained unit. A poem written according to this principle consists of a number of lines which, while all being related to a leading idea, leads to a summing-up, rather than to a flowing narrative.

Arab poets may simplify the structure by using unadorned forms of enumeration. One such form is a string of nouns, adjectives or verbs with nothing in between but copula, filling one or two verse-lines. Other forms are a series of parallel constructions or a series of clauses, which all have the same subject or the same predicate. The varieties occurring in Nu'aymah's poetry can all be traced back to the work of Arab poets, both ancient and modern. Nor is the fact that Nu'aymah makes use of enumerations uncommon; what is unusual is that he employed them so frequently and so lavishly. The emphasis inherent in such summing-up makes his poetry at times less of a whisper than the title of his collection of poems suggests.

[30] *Hams al-ǧufūn*, p. 102-107. The translated lines are from p. 102.

A simple listing may be found in stanzas six, seven and eight of "To M.D.B." [31] the sixth of which runs as follows

Anā fī layliki 'l-qamarū
anā fī ṣafwiki 'l-kadarū
anā fī shadwiki 'n-nadbū
wa fī tanwāḥiki 'sh-shadwū
anā bi-zinādiki 'sh-shararū

"I am the moon in your night
I am the speck on your purity
I am the plaint in your song
and the song in your lament
I am the spark in your silex"

The fourth of the six stanzas of "Yā rafīqī" [32] (O, Companion) consists of twelve verbs in the same person and number in a total of eleven lines. The fifth stanza contains another nine verbs of the same form. A similar form of enumeration is found in "Ḥablu 't-tamannī" [33] (The Rope of Wishing). One of the longest enumerations occurs in "Ibtihālāt" [34] the first six stanzas of which run as follows :

Kaḥḥili 'llāhumma 'aynayyā
bī-shu'ā'in min ḍiyākā
kay tarākā

fī ğamī'i 'l-khalqi; fī dūdi 'l-qubūr
fī nusūri 'l-ğawwi, fī mawği 'l-biḥār
fī ṣahārīği 'l-barārī, fī 'z-zuhūr
fī 'l-kalā, fī't-tibri, fī ramli 'l-qafār

fī qurūḥi 'l burṣi, fī waǧhi 's-salīm
fī yadi 'l-qātili, fī na'shi 'l-qatīl [35]

---

31 *Hams al-ğufūn*, p. 106.
32 *Hams al-ğufūn*, p. 78.
33 *Hams al-ğufūn*, p. 22-25.
34 *Hams al-ğufūn*, p. 35-39. The translated lines are from p. 35 f. With regard to the number of elements in this enumeration, Nu'aymah is surpassed by Īlīyā Abū Māḍī, whose poem "al-Khamr wa 'd-dunyā" (The Wine and the World) in *al-Khamā'il* (The Woods), Beirut, 1965[6], p. 92-94, contains an enumeration of 26 elements.
35 The Arabic text of this and the following line seems to be confused. Instead of *fī nağ'i 'l-qatīl* and *fī na'shi 'l-faṭīm* we have read *fī na'shi 'l-qatīl* and *fī nağ'i 'l-faṭīm.*

fī sarīri 'l-'irsi, fī nağ'i 'l-faṭīm
fī yadi 'l-muḥsini, fī kaffi 'l-bakhīl

Fī fu'ādi 'sh-shaykhi, fī rūḥī 'ṣ-ṣaghīr
fī 'ddi'ā 'l-'ālimi, fī ğahli 'l-ğahūl
fī ghinā 'l-muthrī, wa fī faqri 'l-faqīr
fī qadhā 'l-'āhiri, fī ṭuhri 'l-batūl

wa idhā mā sāwarathā saktatu 'n-nawmi 'l-'amīq
fa'ghmiḍi 'llāhumma ğafnayhā ilā an tastafīq

"Anoint, O Lord, my eyes
with the rays of Thy light
that I may see Thee

In the whole creation : in the worm of the grave,
in the eagles of the sky, in the waves of the sea,
in the cisterns of the land, in the flowers,
in the grass, in the gold-dust, in the sand of the deserts,

In the wounds of the lepers, in the face of the healthy man,
in the hand of the killer, in the bier of the killed,
in the nuptial bed, in the gruel of the weaned,
in the hand of the benefactor, in the palm of the miser,

In the heart of the elder, in the spirit of the younger,
in the pretense of the learned, in the unawareness of the ignorant,
in the richness of the wealthy, in the poverty of the poor,
in the filth of the adulterer, in the purity of the maiden.
And when the silence of the deep sleep converses with them
close down, O Lord, their lids until they awake".

Less conspicuous forms of enumeration occur in "Law tudriku 'l-ashwāk" [36] (If Thorns Would Understand). The fourteen stanzas of this poem consist of monologues directed to a cup-bearer, a lute-player, a castle-owner, a mourner-between-the-graves, a miser and a preacher. One by one the poet asks them to do as they are wont to do, but to leave him to his musings. The first stanza of this poem is interesting in that it is an antistrophe to the wine-song that flourished in the so-called classical period of Arabic literature. The first line is reminiscent of the Arabic opening verse of a poem by the Persian poet Ḥāfiẓ :

[36] *Hams al-ğufūn*, p. 28-34.

Alā yā ayyuhā 's-sāqī adir ka'san wa nāwilhā

Paraphrased by A. J. Arberry as

"Ho, saki, haste the beaker bring
Fill up, and pass it round the ring" [37]

Compare with this Nuʿaymah's stanza :

Ya sāqiya 'l-ğallāsi bi 'llāhi lā
taḥfil bi kāsiya bayna hādhī 'l-ku'ūs
Atriʿ li-ghayrī 'l-kāsa ammā anā
fa 'ḥsub ka'annī lastu bayna 'l-ğulūs
waʿbir wa daʿnī fārigha 'l-kāsī

O, cupbearer of the companions, by God
do not fill my cup between these cups,
pass the cup to someone else. As for me,
reckon as if I were not among the company;
pass on and leave me with an empty cup".

The poem "Lammā ra'aytu 'n-Nās" [38] (After I had seen Mankind) consists of twenty lines, the first ten of which have their parallels in the second ten lines. Moreover, there is a thematic similarity between the two halves of the poem.

Sometimes the enumerated elements consist of pairs of extreme opposites, suggesting all-inclusiveness on more than one score. The above-quoted stanzas of "Ibtihālāt" [39] (Supplications) may serve as an example. The second halves of the first three lines of stanza number two form pairs with the beginning of the consecutive lines. Additionally, the fourth line comprises a pair not extending into another line. The following two stanzas consist of lines which each contain one pair of opposites.

"Awrāqu 'l-kharīf" [40] (Autumn Leaves), a poem of four stanzas, opens with an enumeration, which is rooted in Arabic practice. As the historiographer would often

---

37 *Fifty Poems of Ḥāfiẓ*. Texts and translations collected and made, introduced and annotated by Arthur J. Arberry, Cambridge, 1947, p. 37 text, and p. 83 English translation. Cf. also his note on p. 139.

38 *Hams al-ğufūn*, p. 71 f.

39 *Hams al-ğufūn*, p. 35-39.

40 *Hams al-ğufūn*, p. 47-49.

do when speaking of a prince, or as the literary critic when writing about a poet, or in other circumstances, the poet opens his address to the falling leaves with a series of epithets [41] :

Tanātharī tanātharī
yā bahǧata 'n-naẓar
yā marqaṣa 'sh-shamsi wa yā
urǧūḥata 'l-qamar
yā urghuna 'l-layli wa yā
qīthārata 's-saḥar
yā ramza fikrin ḥā'irī
wa rasma rūḥin thā'irī
yā dhikra maǧdin ghābirī
qad 'āfaka 'sh-shaǧar
tanātharī! tanātharī!

"Fall off - fall off
O, joy of the eye
O, ballroom of the sun and O,
swing of the moon
O, organ of the night and O,
guitar of the morning
O, symbol of a dispairing thought
O, memory of the past glory
the tree has cast you off
fall off! fall off!

Nu'aymah's pantheistic creed and his belief in the reincarnation of the individual soul until its final integration into the all-soul, found expression in many of his poems.

---

[41] Nu'aymah himself writes in this way about Nasīb 'Arīḍah at the end of his review of the latter's volume of poetry *al-Arwāḥ al-ḥā'irah* (Perplexed Spirits) in *al-Ghirbāl*, p. 127-144 : "... among them is the poet of the dumb, and the eloquent, and the lonesome, and the suffering, and the doubting, and the ascetic, and the mystic, and the guided and the guiding perplexity — Nasīb 'Arīḍah. Nu'aymah's review of Ǧibrān's book *al-'Awāṣif* (The Tempests) ended, according to him in the biography of Ǧibrān, with : "... is the poet of the Night of Solitude, the Poet of Loneliness and Melancholy, the poet of Longing and Spiritual Awakening, the poet of the Sea and the Tempest — Gibran Kahlil Gibran (Mīkhā'īl Nu'aymah, *Ǧibrān Khalīl Ǧibrān*, Beirut, 1960[4], p. 164 and Mikhail Naimy, *Kahlil Gibran*, p. 160, Beirut, 1965, second printing of the Beirut edition. The first English edition was published in 1950, New York). The quoted lines do not occur in the review as published in *al-Ghirbāl*, Beirut, 1964[7], p. 218-243.

Against the background of his beliefs a poem such as "aṭ-Ṭarīq" [42] (The Road) becomes more intelligible :

Naḥnu yā 'bnī 'askarun qad tāha fī qafrin saḥīq
narghabu 'l-'awda wa lā nadhkuru min ayna 'ṭ-ṭarīq
fa 'ntasharnā fī ğihāti 'l-qafri nastağlī 'l-athar
nas'alu 'sh-shamsa 'ani 'd-darbi wa nastaftī 'l-ḥağar
wa sanabqā nafḥaṣu 'l-āthāra min hadhā wa dhāk
raythamā nudriku anna 'd-darba fīnā lā hunāk
wa sanabqā fī 'ntiqālin wa shaqā'in wa 'adhāb
wa ṣu'ūdin wa hubūṭin wa dhahābin wa iyāb
wa sanabqā nahğa'u 'l-layla wa fī 's-ṣubḥi nufīq
raythamā nalqā manānā — raythamā nalqā 'ṭ-ṭarīq

"We are, my son, an army roaming in a deep desert
wishing to return, but not remembering the road.
We spread in all directions to find a track
asking the sun about the road, interrogating the stone.
We will go on investigating traces here and there
until we understand that the road is in us, not there.
We will remain fluctuating and in pain and supplication,
going up and down and going and coming.
We will continue to sleep at night and to awaken in the morning
until we meet our sort — until we find the road."

The pantheistic element is present also in the fiftheenth of the eighteen stanzas of "at-Tā'ih" [43] (The Wanderer) in lines which remind one of Omar Khayyam :

a khāliqī raḥmākā — *bi mā barat yadākā!*
in lam akun ṣadākā — *fa ṣawtu man anā?*

"O My Creator have mercy — upon the creation of Thine hands!
If I am not Thine echo — whose voice may I be then"?

Nu'aymah's esteem of official religion has apparently never been very high. This attitude is reflected, for example, in the poem "Law tudriku 'l-ashwāk" [44] (If Thorns Would Understand) in its eleventh and twelfth stanzas :

---

[42] *Hams al-ğufūn*, p. 46.
[43] *Hams al-ğufūn*, p. 54, lines 1 and 2 from top.
[44] *Hams al-ğufūn*, p. 33, lines 1-5 from bottom and p. 34 lines 1-5 from top.

Yā ḥāmila 'l-inğīli yad'ū ilā
nabdhi 'l-ma'āṣī mundhiran bi'l-'iqāb
bashshir wa khalliṣ yā akhī anfusā
ḍallat likay talqā ğamīla 'th-thawāb
idh yanṣabu 'd-dayyānu mīzānahū

Immā ṣamamtu 'l-udhna 'anka falā
taghḍab wa da'nī fī ḍalālī ahīm
idh lī fu'ādun qad ḥawā ğannatā
wa 'llāhu adrā kam ḥawā min ğaḥīm
fakraz, wa da' qalbī wa adrānahū

"O bearer of the gospels who summons us
to do away with sins, warning of punishments,
bring good news and, O, my brother, set free souls
that go astray, that they receive a fine reward
when the Supreme Judge sets up his scales.

When I close my ear on you do not
get angry and let me go wrong in my errors,
because my heart contains a paradise,
and God knows best how many hells;
preach and leave alone my heart with its impurities"

The break with official religion is the subject also of the poem "Ṣadā 'l-ağrās" [45] (The Voice of the Church-bells), in which the church bells summon to prayer. "This sound reminds the poet musing about his youthful years of the woods where he and his comrades used to go instead of to church. The memories and the dingdong of the bells lift him to exstatic heights making him exclaim : "I am the master of the world and of time ..." The poet tumbles down from this state of exstasis when the sound of the church-bells dies out and memories dwindle [46]. The eighth to eleventh stanza or the last four stanzas of the poem give expression to the exstatic feelings of the poet and his consequent relapse [47] :

---

[45] *Hams al-ğufūn*, p. 40-45.

[46] Iḥsān 'Abbās and Muḥammad Yūsuf Nağm, *al-Shi'r al-'arabī fī al-mahğar, Amīrkā al-shamāliyyah* (Arabic Emigrant Poetry, North America), Beirut (1967), p. 125-126. See also Chapter 3 : "al-Ghāb" (The Woods), p. 71-87, which discusses the special significance of "The Woods" in the poetry of the Arab emigrant poets in North America in general. Thoreau's *Walden*, however, gives nature a role of its own, whereas Nu'aymah uses it here as a spiritual stimulus only.

[47] *Hams al-ğufūn*, from p. 43, line 10 from top until the end of the poem on p. 45.

hā hum atrābī qad saraḥū
fī 'l-ghābi yaqūduhumu 'l-maraḥū
wa baqītu anā waḥdī sakrā[nan [48]
yarqaṣu fī qalbī 'l-faraḥū
fa-ğalastu ʿalā katfi 'n-nahrī
mā bayna 'l-ʿawsaği wa 'z-zahrī
al-ʿālamu mamlakatī wa anā
Sulṭānu 'l-ʿālami wa 'd-dahrī
az-zahru yuʿaṭṭiru anfāsī
wa 'n-nahru yuwallidu fī rāsī
asbāḥan rāqiṣatan li-kharī[ri
'l-mā'i wa ṣawti 'l-ağrāsī
din — din — din ...

man dhālika bayna 'l-ashğārī
yamshī ka-khayālin min nārī?
huwa yaḍrabu ʿūdan wa 'l-ashğā[ru
ta'innu li-shakwā 'l-awtārī
din — din ...

az-zahru yunakkisu tīğānah
wa 'l-ḥawru yulamlimu aghṣānah
wa 'r-rīḥu tamurru ʿalā awtā[ri
'l-ʿūdi fa-takhnuqu alḥānah
din ...

Mā bālu sakīnatiya 'ḍṭarabat
wa ğaḥāfilu ashbāḥī harabat
wa 'l-ghābu wa mā fīhā wa wuğū[hu
rifāqī ʿan ʿaynī 'ḥtağabat
qad ʿāda 'sh-shakku wa anṣāruh
ālāmu 'l-ʿayshi wa awzāruh
wa aṭallū min qalbī li-yaraw
qalban tataqaṭṭaʿu awtāruh
wa shabāban yağmaʿuhā abadā
wa yuʿaqqiduhā ʿaqdan ʿaqdā
wa ʿalayhā yaʿzifu alḥānā
lā tuṭribu fī 'd-dunyā aḥadā

[48] The last syllable belongs metrically to the following line. The metrical relation has been indicated by a bracket to separate it from the line with which it has the narrower linguistic relation. The other brackets in the transcript serve a similar purpose.

"Look, my friends roam
in the woods, liveliness leading them.
I remained alone—drunk,
joy dancing in my heart.
I set myself on the river bank
between the box-thorn and the flower;
the world is my kingdom and I am
the Sultan of the world and of time.
The flower perfumes my breathings,
and the river gives birth in my heart
to shapes that dance to the murmur
of the water and to the voice of the bells
ding — ding — ding

Who is it between the trees that
walks like a spectre of fire?
he strums the lute and the trees
sigh at the complaint of the strings
ding — ding

The flower lowers its crown,
the poplar gathers its branches,
and the wind passes over the strings
of the lute and smothers its song.
ding

Why has my inner peace been disturbed,
and have the armies of shapes taken flight;
have the woods and what's in them, the faces of
my comrades disappeared from my eye?
Doubt has returned and its helpers;
the pains and the burdens of life.
They look out from my heart to see
a heart whose strings have been cut,
and a youth taking them together again and again
fastening them with knot after knot
and playing songs on them
not pleasant to anybody in the world".

Nu'aymah's belief in the vegetative function of death has found expression in a poem like "Qubūrun tadūr" [49] (Graves revolve). The first of its seven stanzas runs as follows :

Halummī! Halummī nuḥayyi 'l-qubūr
wa namtaṣṣi minhā raḥīqa 'd-duhūr
'asānā idhā mā ra'aynā 'iẓāmā
yufattiqu minhā 'r-rabī'u 'z-zuhūr
'arafnā bi-anna 'l-fanā'a baqā'ū
wa anna 'l-ḥayāta qubūrun tadūr

"Come on! Come on, lets greet the graves
and sip from them the wine of times;
perhaps we see bones
from which spring has made the flowers burst,
that we know that to pass away is to remain
and that life is graves revolving".

Another source of inspiration for Nu'aymah was his relation with his landlady Bella [50]. This relation found expression in poems which speak of the tension that arose between the heart and the brain as the respective seats of feeling and reason. It is typical of Nu'aymah's moralizing attitude that he did not devote one poem to his partner exclusively, but always to their relation. The poet tries to ease his partner's conscience in "Yā rafīqī" [51] (O, Companion), by asserting that their relation is beyond human concepts of sin, as it is beyond the codes of formal religion. We quote the first seven and the last six lines, which could be considered as forming the first and last stanza of this poem of 57 lines, divided over six stanzas :

Yā rafīqī, rafīqa ğismī wa rūḥī
wa sharīkī fī ni'matī wa shaqā'ī
wa ṣadīqī, ṣadīqa 'ilmī wa ğahlī
wa nadīmī fī shiddatī wa rakhā'ī
in da'ānā rabbu 's-samā'i ilayhī
li-ḥisābin, ḥidhāri min an turā'ī
yā rafīqī amāma rabbi 's-samā'ī

and the last stanza :

---

[49] *Hams al-ğufūn*, p. 68-70.
[50] *Cf.* Ch. II, p. 38 f.
[51] *Hams al-ğufūn*, p. 75-80.

yā rafīqī, rafīqa ğismī wa rūḥī
wa sharīkī fī ni'matī wa shaqā'ī
qul, ra'aynā ṭahāratan wa ğamālā
lā fasādan fī ṣan'i rabbi 's-samā'ī
fa abaḥnā li 'n-nafsi kulla munāhā
wa taraknā 'l-ḥarāma li 'l-fuqahā'ī

"O, my companion, companion of my body and my soul,
partner in my well-being and in my distress
my friend — friend of my knowing and my ignorance,
my confidant in adversity and in my opulence,
when the Lord of Heaven calls us to Him
to answer — beware that you do not dissimulate,
O, my companion, before the Lord of Heaven"

and the sixth stanza :

"O, my companion, companion of my body and my soul,
partner in my well-being and in my distress
say : We saw purity and beauty
not wickedness in the makings of the Lord of Heaven;
we permitted the soul all its wishes
and we left the forbidden to the scribes"

The poet returns to his inner life in the poem "at-Tā'ih" [52] (The Wanderer), describing what the fire of love wrought in his soul. The poem describes the mental state of the poet, but does not deal with any of the outward causes whatsoever. The first five of the eighteen stanzas of this poem run as follows :

Asīru fī ṭarīqī	*fī mahmahin saḥīqī*
wa waḥdatī rafīqī	*wa wağhatī 'l-faḍā*
maṭiyyatī 't-turābū	*wa khawdhatī 's-saḥābū*
wa dir'iya 's-sarābū	*wa rā'idī 'l-qaḍā*
tasūqunī 'th-thawānī	*fī mawkibi 'z-zamānī*
wa lastu adrī shānī	*fī ma'riḍi 'l-warā*
fa lā 'l-qaḍā yanbīnī	*wa lā 'r-rağā yahdīnī*
wa lā 's-samā ta'ṭīnī	*nūran likay arā*
bal fī ḍulū'ī nārū	*tuthīruhā l-aqdārū*
yā laytahā takhtārū	*siwāya mawqidā*

[52] *Hams al-ğufūn*, p. 52-54.

"I travel along my way in a deep desert;
loneliness is my companion and my direction space.
The earth is my steed, and the clouds are my helmet,
the mirage is my armour and fate is my guide.
The seconds drive me on in the train of time;
I do not know my affair in the spectacle of man,
for fate does not inform me, nor does hope lead me,
nor does heaven give me light that I may see.
On the contrary, within me is a fire which fate is kindling.
O, had it chosen somebody else as a fireplace!"

The conflict between the heart and the head is the subject of poems such as "Takhdīru afkār" [53] (Thoughts' Drugging), "Afāqa 'l-qalb" [54] (The Heart Awoke) and "Lammā ra'aytu 'n-nās" [55] (After I had seen Mankind). "Akhī" [56] (My Brother) stands on its own in this volume. Its subject and tone set it apart from the other poems. It is the only nationalistic poem by Nuʿaymah, at least the only one so far known. The point of reference is the great famine from which the people of Mount Lebanon suffered during World War I. Nuʿaymah does not blame the Turks who had forbidden all traffic between Mount Lebanon and the fertile plain of al-Biqāʿ. The mountain people were cut off from the supplies on which they depended, especially after the locust plague of 1915. Instead of pointing his finger at the Turks, Nuʿaymah, in the fourth of the five stanzas of this poem, lays the responsibility for the catastrophe on the Lebanese themselves because they let it happen :

Akhī qad tamma mā law lam nasha'hu naḥnu mā tammā
wa qad ʿamma 'l-balā'u wa law aradnā naḥnu mā ʿammā
fa-lā tandub, fa-udhnu 'l-ghayri lā tuṣghī li-shakwānā
bali 'tbaʿnī li-naḥfira khandaqan bi 'r-rafshi wa 'l-miʿwal
nuwārī fīhi mawtānā

"My brother, something has happened which, if we had not willed it it would not have happened.
Affliction was general — if we had not willed it it would not have been so,
therefore, do not lament — the others will not listen to our complaint
but follow me to dig a trench with spade and pike
to hide in it our dead".

---

53 *Hams al-ǧufūn*, p. 50-51.
54 *Hams al-ǧufūn*, p. 55-63, pp. 57 and 58 have been used for an illustration.
55 *Hams al-ǧufūn*, p. 71-72.
56 *Hams al-ǧufūn*, p. 14-15.

The fifth stanza is still sharper in its abuse. The poet advises the survivors to bury themselves to free the world of their shame and their stench.

Nu'aymah's concept of poetry as the language of the soul is similar to the one held by the poets of the Egyptian romantic movement in the first half of this century. He differs with at least some of them in being less emotional and more contemplative. He sometimes even strikes a rational tone, though the opposite is not absent either. The poem "Dhammuka 'l-ayyām" [57] (Your Reproach of the Days = (Fate) is notable for the poet's love for popular rationalisations, as will appear from the following full quotation :

Dhammuka 'l-ayyāma lā yanfa'uk
fahya lā udhna lahā tasma'uk
lā wa lā 'ayna tarā 'aqraban
fī dayāğīri 'l-asā talsa'uk
lā wa lā qalba yariqqu wa in
ğaffa min ṭūli 'l-bukā madma'uk
'indahā siyyāni yā ṣāḥibī
azharat am aqfarat arbu'uk
'indahā siyyāni yā ṣāḥibī
naghmatu 'l-hāziğī wa 'n-nādibī
wa 'btisāmu 'ṭ-ṭifli fī mahdihī
wa 'ntiḥābu 'l-'āğizi 'l-khā'ibī
wa riḍā 'r-rāḍī bi-qismatihā
wa 'adā'i 'th-thā'iri 'ṣ-ṣākhibī
'adluhā fī annahā lā tarā
ḥāla maghlūbin wa lā ghālibī
dhammuka 'l-'ayyāma lā yanfa'uk
innamā 'l-ayyāmu lā tasma'uk
fahya minka 'ẓ-ẓillu yā ṣāḥibī
'ağaban ẓilluka kam yakhda'uk!

"Your reproach of the days will not avail you
they have no ear to hear you,
no — and no eye to see the scorpion
in the darkness of pain sting you,
no — and no heart softening, even
if your eyes dried out through prolonged weeping.
It is equal to them, O my friend,

[57] *Hams al-ğufūn*, p. 81-82.

whether your quarters are flowery or a desert,
Equal to them, O my friend,
is the song of the joyous and of the mourner,
the smile of the infant in his cradle
and the sigh of the frustrated aged,
the satisfaction of him who is content with what they allotted,
and the enmity of the shouting rebel;
their justice is that they do not see
the state of the vanquished and of the victor;
your reproach of the days will not avail you
because the days do not hear you.
They are your shadow, O my friend.
Astonishing how your shadow deceives you!"

Other poems appealing to reason are "aṭ-Ṭarīq" [58] (The Road), "Qubūrun tadūr" [59] (Graves revolve) and, in a way, "Ya rafīqī" [60] (O my companion), which instructs the partner what to say before the Suppreme Judge to unnerve His arguments. "Takhdīru afkār" [61] (Thoughts' Drugging), reflecting Nuʿaymah's love relation with Bella, on the other hand, is an outburst against reason. The lines 18 through 24 of this 24-line poem run as follows :

Bi-rabbiki afkārī daʿīniya sābiḥā
bi-baḥri wuğūdī — dūdatan bayna asmākī
ḍarīran, aṣamman, abkaman, mutağalbibā
bi-ğahlī wa ḍaʿfī, dūna ʿilmin wa idrākī
fa-naṣḥuki tamwīhun wa ṣidquki ḥabbatū
mina 'l-qamḥi fī akdāsi tibnin wa aḥsākī
wa kam ṣaddaqat tamwīhaki 'n-nafsu sābiqā
fa-mā kāna aghbāhā wa mā kāna aqsākī!

"By your Lord, my thoughts, let me drift
in the sea of my existence — a worm between the fishes
blind — deaf — mute — clad with
my ignorance and weakness — without knowledge and perception
your advice is delusion — and your sincerity
a grain of wheat between heaps of straw and chaff.

58 *Hams al-ğufūn*, p. 46.
59 *Hams al-ğufūn*, p. 68-70.
60 *Hams al-ğufūn*, p. 75-80.
61 *Hams al-ğufūn*, p. 50-51.

> How often in former times the soul believed your falseness;
> how stupid it was — and how severe you were".

Though small in size, Nu'aymah's volume of poetry is not uninteresting. It demonstrates the transition from traditional to modern forms, and it reveals a temperate emotion through the lines.

IV. THE LITERARY WORK : NARRATIVE PROSE

Nuʿaymah's narrative prose comprises a wide diversity of writings, which, for convenience sake, can be grouped together under the headings : novels, stories and biographical works.

The novels, *Mudhakkarāt al-Arqash* (The Memoirs of Pitted Face) [1], *Liqā'* (Encounter) [2] and *The Book of Mirdad* (n.pr., The One who Returns) [3], were all published shortly after the Second World War, but parts of the *Mudhakkarāt al-Arqash* had been published in serialized form in the Arabic magazine *al-Funūn* (The Arts), New York, in 1917 and 1918. The latest novel is *al-Yawm al-akhīr* (The Last Day), first published in 1963 [4].

From 1914 onward Nuʿaymah has written more than 80 stories, the majority of which have been collected in the volumes *Kān mā kān* (Once Upon a Time) [5], *Akābir*

---

1 First published in book form, Beirut, 1949. For references the third edition, Beirut, 1962, has been used. The book was translated into English and published in New York, 1952, according to information by the author, in *Sabʿūn* III, p. 219, with the title *Memoirs of a Vagrant Soul.*

2 *Liqā'* (Encounter). First edition, Beirut, 1946. All references are to the fifth edition, Beirut, 1964. An English translation (by the author) of *Liqā'* and of twelve other stories was published in Bangalore, 1957, with the title *Till we meet...*

3 Published originally in English, Beirut, 1948. Nuʿaymah, *Sabʿūn* III, p. 219, mentions an English edition published in New York, 1950. The English edition of 1962, London, lists the Beirut edition of 1948 and a Bombay edition of 1954. An Arabic translation by the author appeared in 1952 in Beirut. For references the fourth Arabic edition, Beirut, 1963, and the English edition, London, 1962, have been used.

4 Parts of this novel were published in four issues of *al-Funūn* : Volume III, issue 3 (October 1917), p. 177-186; 4 (November 1917), p. 255-274; 5 (May 1918), p. 320-333; 6 (June 1918), p. 427-440. These texts have undergone some alterations, the most significant of which were the cutting out of a few characters, as al-Signor, Milḥ al-Arḍ (Salt of the Earth), the Phonograph and three Syrian journalists who all received their share of contempt in the original version. The philosophical passages underwent some changes also, and several provocative lines have been omitted, such as Vol. III, issue 5, p. 322 :

"I and the Father are one
I and the Son are one
I and the Father are one likewise. This undoubtedly is a heresy no human religion will forgive". Disregarding the excisions the original text did not reach a length equal to half the present novel. What has been kept of the original text is no more than one third of the finished work.

5 First edition, Beirut, 1937. References are to the 6th edition, Beirut, 1963.

(Notables) [6], *Abū Baṭṭah* (The Fat-Calved Man) [7], and *Hawāmish* (Marginals) [8]. Some twenty odd stories have been strewn in between non-narrative prose over the collections *al-Marāḥil* (Stages) [9], *al-Bayādir* (The Threshing Floors) [10], *Ṣawt al-'ālam* (The Voice of the World) [11], *Fi mahabb al-rīḥ* (Windward) [12] and *Durūb* (Roads) [13].

The play *al-Ābā' wa al-banūn* (Fathers and sons) [14] is considered within the context of the narrative prose. Its early creation and some aspects of its story make it an interesting part of Nu'aymah's literary production. What role it played in the development of the Arabic theater, however, has not been studied here.
Nu'aymah is at his best as a narrator in his Autobiography [15], but this work, as has been indicated, will be dealt with together with his Biography of Ğibrān [16] in the following chapter.

With regards to his subject-matter Nu'aymah stands aside the mainstream of the Arabic novel as it developed from Ḥusayn Haykal's *Zaynab* [17] onward. Instead of dealing with issues of social significance, as do the early Arabic novels, and instead of depicting scenes of local colour, Nu'aymah's novels all view human life from a cosmic perpective. In the *Mudhakkarāt al-Arqash*, as well as in *Liqā'*, the main characters try to reach out above their earthly existence. They show themselves obsessed by ideals of purity which do not fall short of Manichaean ideals of perfection. Al-Arqash, who is represented as having written the *Mudhakkarāt* (Memoirs), is so preoccupied with his chastity, that he rather kills his newly wed bride than succumb

---

6 First edition, Beirut, 1956. References are to the second edition, Beirut, 1963.
7 First edition, Beirut, 1959. References are to the second edition, Beirut, 1963.
8 First edition, Beirut, 1965.
9 First edition, Beirut, 1932. References are to the fourth edition, Beirut, 1966.
10 First edition, Cairo, 1945. References are to the fifth edition, Beirut, 1963.
11 First edition, Cairo, 1948. References are to the third edition, Beirut, 1961.
12 First edition, Beirut, 1953. References are to the third edition, Beirut, 1962.
13 First edition, Beirut, 1954. References are to the fourth edition, Beirut, 1966.
14 The play was serialized in the Arabic magazine *al-Funūn* in New York, Volume 2, issues 7 (December 1916), p. 609-622; 8 (January 1917), p. 710-726; 9 (February 1917), p. 794-813; 10 (March 1917), p. 905-930; 11 (December 1917), p. 1002-1023. It was published in book form in New York in 1917. For references the third edition, Beirut, 1962 has been used.
15 *Sab'ūn. Ḥikāyat 'umr* (Seventy. A Life Story), in three volumes, Beirut, 1959-1960.
16 *Ğibrān Khalīl Ğibrān. Ḥayātuhu, mawtuhu, adabuhu, fannuhu* (Ğibrān Khalīl Ğibrān. His Life, His Death, His Literature, His Art). First Arabic edition, Beirut, 1934. An English edition by the author was published in New York, 1950, with the title *Kahlil Gibran. His Life and His Work.*
17 *Zaynab* is generally considered the first real novel in Egyptian literature. It was published in 1913, and not in 1914, as has been convincingly demonstrated by Hamdi Sakkut, *The Egyptian Novel and its Main Trend. From 1913 to 1952.* Cairo, 1971, p. 12. The second edition of *Zaynab* dates from 1929. Until then the novel had been comparatively unknown.

to temptation, taking, to the extreme as it were, Christ's advice to cut off a seducing hand or foot and to pluck out a wicked eye.

Leonardo in *Liqā'* flees human society to cleanse himself of the last remnants of sexual longing in order to effect a spiritual union with the girl he loves. They both die in the process, but here it is spontaneous death which forms the climax and proof of the new symbiosis. Remarkable is the complete passivity of the girl, who is unconscious from the moment Leonardo makes his first attempt to play the soul-uniting melody on his violin until he succeeds in his efforts, after a period of self-imposed withdrawal.

Mirdād (The One Who Returns), a kind of Christ reincarnate, guides an assembly of monks who, in their turn, as the biblical disciples, go out into the world to preach the gospel they have received. No doubt, Nu'aymah in conceiving this novel was inspired by Ǧibrān's *Prophet* [18], which in its turn shows the influence of Nietzsche's *Zarathustra*. The success of these two books may have induced Nu'aymah to create a divine teacher of his own [19].

Nu'aymah's latest novel *al-Yawm al-akhīr* (The Last Day) [20] came out in 1963. It is the account of one day in the life of Dr. Mūsā al-'Askarī, the main character, who has been told by a mysterious voice at midnight that the coming day would be his last. In the course of the day the main character comes to perceive the utter futility of his earthly concerns and occupations, and turns into another man. The change, however, is effected only after a stream of events which all tax his feelings to the utmost. His mute son addresses him and miraculously overcomes a paralysis of the legs; the only son of the mayor of the village dies at the age of three; the otherwordly messenger, who had announced the beginning of the last day, presents himself disguised as a beggar at the door of the main character; his gardener discovers a pot filled with golden coins in the fruitgarden up in the mountains, but Mūsā al-'Askarī not wanting the treasure donates it to the gardener, who again does not accept it; on the way back from the fruitgarden Mūsā al-'Askarī is witness to an accident with a shot-gun injuring a birdhunter. He returns to the garden and asks

[18] First edition, New York, 1923. Nu'aymah wrote in the biography of Ǧibrān : "He created a mouthpiece called 'Almustafa' endowing him with a soul so enlightened that his hearer called him 'Prophet of God' ". The very name 'Prophet' impresses with dignity and inspires reverence. A word said by a man clothed in prophetic majesty carries much more weight and magnitude than when said by a common man". Quotation from the second English edition, Beirut, 1965, p. 186.

[19] Virginia Hilu, *Beloved Prophet. The love letters of Kahlil Gibran and Mary Haskell and her private journal*, London, 1972. She writes that until 1970 four million copies of *the Prophet* had been sold and that the book still sells at a rate of 7000 copies per week (p. 4). On the subject of these love-letters *cf.* Ch. V, note 29.

[20] First edition, Beirut, 1963.

the gardener to help him bring the wounded man to a hospital; they notify the police; and both are taken into custody on suspicion of man-slaughter. They are released only after the wounded man has regained his consciousness and has affirmed their innocence. Back home he hears that his son has left with a man who calls himself "The Unnamed"; he has a dream in which he sees the Unnamed together with his son rowing upstream on the river time; he goes to the airport to meet his wife who had previously eloped to Switzerland, but had cabled that day that she would return the same evening. The plane crashes while landing and burns out. At home he finds a second cable informing him that his wife had missed the plane, but in the course of the day he has reached a state of serenity, making him imperturbable. His old life has ended and a new life lies ahead of him.

Liqā' (Encounter), *The Book of Mirdad* and *al-Yawm al-akhīr* resemble *Pilgrim's Progress* in so far as they depict the struggle of a man with all kinds of negative forces in an effort to reach a higher plane of being. But Nu'aymah's heroes are not fighting personifications of evil, and are not clad in allegorical arms and apparel like Bunyan's Christian. Like *Pilgrim's Progress*, and also like the moral novels so well-known in European literature, Nu'aymah's novels are meant to instruct more than to divert. Commenting on his *Mudhakkarāt al-Arqash* (The Memoirs of Pitted Face), Nu'aymah states that he began writing this novel "without plan or concept other than the persistent wish to create a person through whose tongue he might express the thoughts accumulating in his mind about the unity of man and God" [21]. A similar statement is made by him with respect to *The Book of Mirdad* [22].

While Nu'aymah considered the novel as a convenient vehicle for his ideas, he also valued the story. A considerable number of his stories are merely expositions moulded into dialogues. Their subjects vary from communism and socialism in "Satastarīḥūna yawm astarīḥ" (You Will Rest the Day I Rest) [23] to spiritual freedom in "al-Ḥakīm wa al-samakah" (The Sage and the Fish) [24], to the purposefulness of human life by demolishing arguments to the contrary in "Nāsif al-'ālam" (The Destroyer of the World) [25]. This wisdom may be spread by any tongue, by an apparition in a dream in "Ḥaddathanī Ǧibrān" (Gibran Told Me) [26]; by a fish in "Al-Ḥakīm wa al-samakah" (The Sage and the Fish); by a crow in "'Iẓat al-ghurāb" (The Sermon of the Crow) [27]; by a lizard in "al-Ḍabb wa al-murashshaḥ wa al-nākhib" (The Lizard,

---

21 *Sab'ūn* III, p. 210.
22 *Sab'ūn* III, p. 214.
23 *Fī mahabb al-rīḥ* (Windward), p. 78-87.
24 *Ṣawt al-'ālam* (The Voice of the World), p. 78-87.
25 *Hawāmish* (Marginals), p. 68-82.
26 *Fī mahabb al-rīḥ* (Windward), p. 158-164.
27 *Al-Marāḥil* (Stages), p. 128-140. This story appears to be a paraphrase of *St Luke* 12, 24.

the Candidate and the Voter) [28]; and even by a grain of wheat in "Ḥabbatān min al-qamḥ" (Two Grains of Wheat) [29].

Nuʿaymah's obvious aim to instruct the reader also resulted in his writing a number of allegories. "Wāḥat al-salām" (Oasis of Peace) [30] is about an oasis which is impenetrable except to those who have overcome the world. The four kings, who each have conquered one quarter of the world, are repulsed, whereas a miserable nobody enters without difficulty because he had freed himself of all earthly longings. "Al-Sayf wa al-qaṣabah" (The Sword and the Pen) [31] relates the battle between sword and pen, in which the latter wins, even after all the pens have been destroyed by burning. A piece of charcoal, the leftover of a pen, is used to write the words which inspire the people to new resistance against the tyranny of the sword. Another allegory is "Ḥikāyat damʿah" (The Tale of a Tear) [32] about a tear which refuses to be shed until its owner apprehends that man can free himself from the bondage of place and time by breaking through its manifold egg-shell coverings.

Nuʿaymah's Greek-Orthodox upbringing, his training for the priesthood, and possibly his experiences in freemasonry could have inspired him with respect to to the story of the finding of the book in *The Book of Mirdad* [33], and to ritualistic stories such as "Qalāmat ẓifr" (Nail-Paring) [34], "Wa yadhūb al-ǧalīd" (The Ice Will Melt) [35] and "Zāwiyah dāfi'ah" (A Warm Recess) [36]. In *The Book of Mirdad* the narrator of the frame story undertakes an arduous journey in quest of the mysterious book. On his journey along a slippery flint slope he is robbed in succession of his provisions, his staff, and his clothes, and he is even not allowed to take shelter for the night in a cave. Naked and without his staff he is left in the dark near a bottomless abyss. Only when he has lost his last earthly support and falls down into the pit is he saved to receive *The Book of Mirdad.* While falling down he hears the words : "Die to live, or live to die" [37]. And the guard of the book eventually tells him : "You have died to live" [38].

---

[28] *Hawāmish* (Marginals), p. 150-159.

[29] *Al-Marāḥil* (Stages), p. 125-127.

[30] *Al-Bayādir* (The Threshing Floors), p. 179-186.

[31] *Fī mahabb al-rīḥ* (Windward), p. 34-42.

[32] *Al-Bayādir* (The Threshing Floors), p. 170-178.

[33] *Kitāb Mirdād, Manārah wa mīnā'*, fourth edition, Beirut, 1963, p. 16-33. English edition, *The Book of Mirdad, A Lighthouse and a Haven*, London, 1962, p. 13-20, Chapter "Flint Slope".

[34] *Abū Baṭṭah* (The Fat-Calved Man), p. 133-142.

[35] *Abū Baṭṭah* (The Fat-Calved Man), p. 97-105.

[36] *Hawāmish* (Marginals), p. 57-61.

[37] *Kitāb Mirdād*, p. 33, *The Book of Mirdad* (English version), p. 20.

[38] *Kitāb Mirdād*, p. 36, *The Book of Mirdad* (English version), p. 22.

"Wa yadhūb al-ğalīd" (The Ice Will Melt) is the title of a story about a woman burning wood piled on the frozen surface of a water reservoir to defrost the icy heart of man. She is said to be not in her right mind, but she knows how to translate her action into perfectly understandable words : "A little mercy and a little forgiveness and the ice will melt everywhere". Sometimes, however, the spell of the ritual is broken and the performer is left alone, exposed in all his madness. The iron-monger in "Qalāmat ẓifr" puts his customer's patience to a hard trial by telling him every two hours to return after two more hours. In the end the iron-monger is found paring his nails, a ritual he performs to rid himself of his sharp edges. He keeps the parings in a box as a reminder of agressions to be curbed. He invites the customer to follow his example. However, when the iron-monger by some inadvertent movement sheds the box with parings over the floor his composure leaves him and utter madness prevails.

The more simple forms of Christianity are apparent in the story of the paralyzed girl, who is miraculously healed, when her parents swallow their pride and start searching for the strange beggar they had chased from their door earlier the same day [39]. A miracle seems to take place in the story "Ğundīyān" (Two soldiers) [40] also. A young peasant, who is the only support of his family, encounters on his way to the recruitment center of the army an invalid soldier with a broken wooden leg and staff, leaning against a tree. Having asked the peasant where he is going, the soldier tries to dissuade him from obeying the summons of the government. The peasant decides to go home and fetch a donkey to carry the soldier, disregarding thereby the appointed hour. When he returns to the spot where the soldier laid, he finds that the wooden leg and broken staff are the only signs of his former presence. The paralyzed boy in "Milād ğadīd" (A Rebirth) [41] has set all his hopes on Jesus to be cured from his illness. When a burglar enters his room through the window, the boy asks who he is and receives "Jesus" for an answer. At the instant bidding of the boy the burglar tells him to walk, and the boy gets up and walks.

Supernatural persons appear in "Aṣfar al-Nāb" (Yellow Teeth) [42] and the story "Hadiyyat al-Ḥayzabūn" (Ḥayzabūn's present) [43], which has to do with black magic. The first story is about an encounter of the narrator with what he holds for an apparition of the beggar, Aṣfar al-Nāb, of whom he had been afraid in his childhood. The beggar is accompanied by the angel of death, Azrael, in the appearance of a boy. Aṣfar al-Nāb whose last hour has sounded, declares himself to be the equal of

39 "'Ābir sabīl" (A Wayfarer), *Akābir* (Notables), p. 43-51.
40 *Abū Baṭṭah* (The Fat-Calved Man), p. 143-151.
41 *Abū Baṭṭah* (The Fat-Calved Man), p. 174-181.
42 *Abū Baṭṭah* (The Fat-Calved Man), p. 124-132.
43 *Abū Baṭṭah* (The Fat-Calved Man), p. 165-173.

any man, since his impending death has made him independent. The story "Hadiyyat al-Ḥayzabūn", using the same theme as Gogol's *Eve of St. John*, relates how a young woman follows the advice of a North African magician, killing her newly born son in order to find a pot filled with gold. She kills the magician after the pot has been found, but then the gold turns into ashes. She tells her story on her deathbed to a young girl, and asks her to let her see the pot for the last time. The ashes regain their golden appearance for a brief moment until the dying woman has expired her last breath.

Several stories in the collection *Hawāmish* (Marginals) likewise refer to otherworldly powers. "Faylasūfat al-ḍay'ah" (The Village Philosopher) [44] relates the story of a sharp-tongued woman who is never slow to ridicule commonplace thought. She tells the wailing women that the child they bury would have lived if God had shown the mercy for which they are praying. Cursed by one of the women for this irreverent talk she becomes mute. In "Ṣabr Ayyūb" (Job's Patience) [45] Job himself appears to imbue the main character, who is pestered all along by his wife, with the patience he prayed for. "Ṣalawāt" (Prayers) [46] may also be included with these stories. It consists of a collection of anecdotes about prayers, which, with supreme illogic, were or were not answered.

Notwithstanding the five years Nu'aymah spent in Russia and the twenty odd years he lived in America, only one of his novels and three of his stories are set outside Lebanon. *Mudhakkarāt al-Arqash* (The Memoirs of Pitted Face) [47] and the story "Sa'ādat al-Bayk" (His Highness the Beg) [48] are located in New York; "Shorty" [49] has France during the First World War as its background; and "'Ulbat kabrīt" (A Box of Matches) [50] compares Lebanese altruism with an example of French stingyness. Stories such as "Sā'at al-kūkū" (The Cuckoo-clock) [51], "al-Bankārūliyā" (corrupt form of Baccalaureate) [52] have to do with Lebanese emigrants, but their setting is the Lebanese mountains which are shown to be preferable, because of the more simple conditions of life which prevail there.

With regard to the social perspective of the stories, Nu'aymah's sympathy is always

---

44 *Hawāmish* (Marginals), p. 26-29.
45 *Hawāmish* (Marginals), p. 47-52.
46 *Hawāmish* (Marginals), p. 96-116.
47 *Cf.* footnote 1 above.
48 *Kān mā kān* (Once Upon a Time), p. 94-103.
49 *Kān mā kān* (Once Upon a Time), p. 104-124.
50 *Akābir* (Notables), p. 106-112.
51 *Kān mā kān* (Once Opon a Time), p. 7-38.
52 *Abū Baṭṭah* (The Fat-Calved Man), p. 71-78.

with the weaker party, be it the wife of the well-to-do merchant ("al-'Āqir", The Barren One) [53], the poor peasants ("Akābir", Notables) [54], an intinerant merchant ("Ṣadīqī 'Abd al-Ghaffār", My friend Abdul-Ghaffār) [55], or the half-wit in "Ṣādiq" (n.pr. "Truthful") [56]. Animals share in Nu'aymah's compassion for the weak, as is demonstrated by the story "al-Ḥakīm wa al-samakah" (The wise man and the fish) [57], in which the fish, while hooked by the wise man, questions the latter's independence when a simple fish is able to keep him ensnared for many hours. "At-Tawbah" (Repentance) [58] relates the conversion of an indomitable hunter after his son has almost died because of a bone in his throat.

In Nu'aymah's philosophy the killing of an animal is no less a crime than a deliberate murder. This point of view forms the basis of "'Uṣfūr wa Insān" (Bird and man) [59] : A good-for-nothing boy kills in rage a highly esteemed youth, when the latter shoots the bird the boy has so patiently trained to eat from his hand. The story merely tells why the boy killed, but not the slightest effort is made to impart this information to those who demand the prosecution of the boy.

A concomitant of this compassion for the weaker partly is the exposure of the stronger. The village Shaykh commits a murder ("Sanatuhā al-ğadīdah", Her New Year) [60]; the landlord and his wife are merciless to their tenants ("Akābir", Notables) [61]; the lawyer, who so much insisted upon the truthfulness of his employee, lies when he comes to grips with the law unhesitatingly sacrificing the simple Ṣādiq to save himself ("Ṣādiq") [62]; the famous poet is a small-minded family tyrant ("'Itāb", Reproach) [63]; and the teacher tries to adorn himself with the laurels his pupil deserves ("Al-Sarnūk", n.pr.) [64].

This rather simplistic patterning of right and wrong, however, has not been stereotyped to the same extent as in Ğibrān's narratives. Nu'aymah, indeed, criticized Ğibrān on this count : "He never portrayed in any of his descriptions a vile shepherd,

---

[53] *Kān mā kān* (Once Upon a Time), p. 52-83.
[54] *Akābir* (Notables), p. 7-16.
[55] *Abū Baṭṭah* (The Fat-Calved Man), p. 117-123.
[56] *Akābir* (Notables), p. 73-80.
[57] *Ṣawt al-'ālam* (The Voice of the World), p. 78-87.
[58] *Abū Baṭṭah* (The Fat-Calved Man), p. 36-44.
[59] *Akābir* (Notables), p. 62-72.
[60] *Kān mā kān* (Once Upon a Time), p. 39-51.
[61] *Akābir* (Notables), p. 7-16.
[62] *Akābir* (Notables), p. 73-80.
[63] *Abū Baṭṭah* (The Fat-Calved Man), p. 27-35.
[64] *Abū Baṭṭah* (The Fat-Calved Man), p. 87-96.

a base peasant, a mean worker, nor a just ruler, a devoted priest, nor a monk with a bit of belief and compassion in his heart, nor did he portray two kindred, loving, happy spouses" [65]. Nuʿaymah certainly works with fewer stereotypes, but they do occur in his stories. The corrupting influence of culture is one of his standard motifs. It occurs in "Akābir" (Notables) [66], in which story the cultivated present landlord is contrasted with his father, an amiable man with whom the tenants shared their food when he came to take his portion of the harvest. The motif occurs also in stories such as "Sāʿat al-kūkū" (The Cuckoo-clock) [67], "Sanatuhā al-ğadīdah" (Her New Year) [68], "al-Bankārūliyā" (The Baccalaureate) [69]. On the whole, however, Nuʿaymah's scapegoats are not so easily classified. Men and women have the same vices, such as greed. The wife in "Ṣabr Ayyūb" (Job's Patience) [70] is so much lured by the prospect of greater profits that she presses her husband not to sell the apples but to leave them on the tree a little longer in order to fetch a better price. A sudden storm puts her dreams to naught. In "Mağānīn" (Mad People) [71] the man makes an unfortunate decision on similar grounds. Poor Sattūt is wrong and not her rich opposite neighbour. Sattūt is so much occupied with stigmatizing the latter as a debauched woman that she forgets her own safety and drowns when she erroneously believes she has discovered the truth ("Maṣraʿ Sattūt", Sattūt's Death) [72]. The man who, like Lady Macbeth, is haunted by unwashable bloodstains on his hands, is earning his daily bread by crushing stones for road construction [73].
Ğibrān's most notable scapegoat, the priest, is hardly present in Nuʿaymah's stories. One of the exceptions is the priest in "al-ʿĀqir" (The Barren One) [74]. The original version of the story, published in the Arabic magazine *al-Funūn* [75], depicts the priest as having wished the couple many children, and as having gone home in the best of spirits because he had pocketed ten pounds. The later version, as published in the volume *Kān mā kān*, does not have these sentences and portrays the priest a kinder and

---

[65] *Al-Mağmuʿah al-kāmilah li-muʾalaffāt Ğibrān Khalīl Ğibrān al-ʿarabiyyah* (The Complete Collection of the Arabic Works of Ğibrān), Beirut, 1964, p. 13. The first words of the quotation in Arabic are : "... *ma sawwar fī kull mā ṣawwar* ...". Likewise he criticized the black and white pattern in "Ilā Tawfīq ʿAwwād fī Al-Ṣabī al-aʿrağ" (To T.A. on "The Crippled Boy"). *Fī al-ghirbāl al-ğadīd* (In the New Sieve). Vol. 7 of the *Mağmūʿah* (Complete works), p. 550.

[66] *Akābir* (Notables), p. 7-16.

[67] *Kān mā kān* (Once Upon a Time), p. 7-38.

[68] *Kān mā kān* (Once Upon a Time), p. 39-51.

[69] *Abū Baṭṭah* (The Fat-Calved Man), p. 71-78.

[70] *Hawāmish* (Marginals), p. 47-52.

[71] *Al-Mağmūʿah al-kāmilah* (The Complete Collection), Vol. 7, Beirut, 1973, p. 329-335.

[72] *Akābir* (Notables), p. 17-25.

[73] "Kassār al-ḥaṣā" (The Stone Crusher), *Akābir* (Notables), p. 26-33.

[74] *Kān mā kān* (Once Upon a Time), p. 52-83.

[75] *Al-Funūn* (The Arts), Vol. II, Issue 4, September 1916, p. 292-321.

a more religious man. The prior in "Thā'irān" (Two Rebels) [76] is a most friendly and harmless man, whose greatest concern is to re-unite the support of the *ancien régime*, the general, and his rebel daughter. The prior of the small religious community in the ark, ominously called Shamadam (= Sham Adam), stands alone in his refusal to follow Mirdad. The other monks recognize the heaven-sent messenger and put his teachings into practice (*The Book of Mirdad*). Otherwise church functionaries are conspicuously absent. *The Book of Mirdad* is rather a criticism of the holy institution when it is turned into an enterprise in its own right. By choosing the Ark of Noah as the sanctuary around which annually two feasts, the Day of the Vine and the Day of the Ark [76a], are celebrated, Nu'aymah has given a more universal meaning to his criticism than e.g. Ǧibrān did in his "Khalid the heretic" [77].

Two early stories should not be passed by without comment. Nu'aymah deals in them with issues which had not been approached in Arabic, and to which Nu'aymah himself never returned again. "al-'Āqir" (The Barren One) [78] has to do with the emancipation of women. But the problem posed by this story has nothing to do with the casting of the veil or the education of women, which found its principal protagonist in Qāsim Amīn [79]. Nu'aymah's story exposes as false the otherwise unquestioned supposition of female barrenness in the case of a childless union. The female partner, called Ǧamīlah, moreover, holds that happiness in marriage is not dependent upon the existence of an offspring, asserting in this way her being a partner in her own right. The other story, "Shorty" (nick-name for a soldier) [80], relates the misery of soldiers in war-time France infected with a venerial disease. These are not great stories. Their aim seems simply to be to knock the meaning into any head. Ǧamīlah in "al-'Āqir" writes a long letter to her husband explaining that another man has made her pregnant and then commits suicide. Shorty dictates a long farewell letter to the narrator, and makes his suicidal approach of the guards. The sentimentality which pervades these stories, however, is of a milder sort than Ǧibrān's in his early prose, and also milder than Haykal's in his *Zaynab*. Tears are not shed and sighs are not heard in "al-'Āqir", because Ǧamīlah does not want the others to notice her affliction. Shorty exerts himself in amusing his fellow patients until the fatal night. Both stories evince a kind of bravery which was not unknown in Europe at that time.

---

76 *Abū Baṭṭah* (The Fat-Calved Man), p. 106-116.

77 *Al-Arwāḥ al-mutamarridah* (Spirits Rebellious), in : *al-Maǧmū'ah al-kāmilah li-mu'alaffāt Ǧibrān Khalīl Ǧibrān al-'arabiyyah* (The Complete Collection of the Arabic Writings of Ǧibrān Khalīl Ǧibrān), Beirut, 1964, p. 121-166.

78 *Kān mā kān* (Once Upon a Time), p. 52-83.

79 Qāsim Amīn, 1856-1908. His *Taḥrīr al-mar'ah* (The Liberation of the Woman, Cairo, 1899) may be considered as the starting point of the emancipation of women in Egypt.

80 "Shorty", *Kān mā kān* (Once Upon a Time), p. 104-124.

Nu'aymah poses the problem of filial obedience when a marriage is arranged by the parents in his play *al-Ābā' wa al-banūn* (Fathers and Sons) [81] thus entering a field in which others, notably Ǧibrān with *al-Ağniḥah al-mutakassirah* (Broken Wings) [82], had preceded him. The development of the story is partly in the style of his time, but it does not lack new elements. The daughter to be given in marriage is part of a family consisting of a mother, the girl and two brothers, one of them older and one of them younger than the girl. The suitor, acceptable to the mother, is the son of a Beg, whose richest days have passed. The son, moreover, is a friend of the bottle, the card-game and a poetaster. The elder brother of the girl has a friend, a young teacher whose sister stays with him during the winter holidays. The brother opposes the marriage of his sister to the son of the Beg, but despairs of success because of the blind obedience of the girl. The friend talks her into some independent thinking, and in due time the engagement is broken off by her. An assault against the life of the teacher and a slander campaign, in which the younger brother of the girl takes part with all his heart, are contrived by the son and his father, the Beg, respectively. The mother, however, does not falter in her decision to have the marriage concluded until the daughter becomes seriously ill, and recovers only through the dedication of the teacher's sister. It is only then that the mother gives in.

Nu'aymah differs from his predecessors in his limitation of adverse events, and in giving the play a happy ending. The discussions, moreover, all function within the framework of the story. The language is simple and sometimes colloquial. In these respects Nu'aymah's story is the antithesis of Ǧibrān's *al-Ağniḥah al-mutakassirah* (Broken Wings) which is characterized by an unhappy ending; a number of excursions which have no function in the story; and overloaded language. To Nu'aymah goes the credit of having dealt with the problem in an unsentimental way, which, indeed, cannot be said of all of his stories, but which makes the present play a rare bird among the fowls of Arabic literature of his time. New in this story is that a church member, the mother of the girl, comes to recognize that freethinkers, — that is to say the young teacher and his sister — are not so bad as she had thought they were. The teacher, moreover, does not denounce the church, as Ǧibrān's freethinkers do, but merely asserts his freedom to have his own beliefs, while demonstrating at the same time that he is not irreligious.

Nu'aymah's technique of story-telling bears witness to his acquaintance with pre-revolutionary Russian prose. His early stories have a more balanced construction

---

[81] *Cf.* p. 114, footnote 14.

[82] First published 1912 in New York.

than the firstlings in fiction of the great authors of his time, such as Maḥmūd Taymūr [83] and Ṭāhā Ḥusayn [84]. The latter frequently leave the main track of their stories and novels, to indulge in some side-line expositions which may or may not have anything to do with the story as such. Nu'aymah's stories develop along a straight line and extraneous matter is not allowed to slip in. The *dénouement* is prepared for in the preceding scenes, but here Nu'aymah does not always escape from being a little over-explicit in the preparation. When a person is on the verge of committing suicide, or is to die through an accident, invariably a number of references to death and dying precede the fatal act. The narrator in "Shorty" writes in his diary before he knows of Shorty's death : "I imagined that death was standing at my side addressing me" [85], and "It was as if I shook hands with death" [86], and "that these beds were nothing but graves containing dead men who had not yet understood that they had died" [87]. The story "Sanatuhā al-ǧadīdah" (Her New Year) is rich in allusions to death and dying before the Shaykh murders his baby-daughter by burying her alive : "The storm *wails* over the *remains* of 1908" [88]. "*Shrouds* of darkness are covering it and the sky is spreading a white carpet over its *grave*..." [89]. The laughter of the youngster is carried away by the wind "to be *buried* in the wadi" [90]. The lights in the houses "*die out*" [91]. "The old year did not *breathe its last*..." [92]. "The storm *wails* and heaven *weeps*" [93]. "The storm resumes its *funeral* procession making him

---

[83] Maḥmud Taymūr, born 1894 in Cairo. His first collection of stories *al-Shaykh Ǧum'ah wa aqāṣīṣ ukhrā'* (Sheikh Ǧum'ah and other stories), Cairo, 1925, established him as a story-writer. He has published more than twenty volumes of stories, novels, plays and literary essays. He has sometimes been called the Egyptian Maupassant. Muḥammad Naǧm (A.U.B.), *al-Qiṣṣah fī al-adab al-'arabī al-ḥadīth*, 3rd impr. Beirut, 1966, p. 309, finds Nu'aymah's stories in *Kān mā kān* on more than one count superior to Taymūr's early stories. He stresses that a strong point in Nu'aymah's stories is his analysis of the human soul, pulsating with the natural throb of life (p. 310).

[84] Ṭāhā Ḥusayn, born 1889 in Upper Egypt, died 1973, was one of the most remarkable literary talents of modern Egypt. Having lost his eyesight in his pre-school years he was nonetheless sent to Cairo at the age of 13 to attend lessons at al-Azhar. Soon, however, he became a student of the newly founded Egyptian University, where he completed his studies with a doctoral thesis in 1914. He then went to study at the Sorbonne, where he received a doctor's degree in 1918. His list of writings is impressive, not only because of its quantity but also on account of its variety. He translated from the Greek and from the French, published studies on Arabic poetry, essays on literary criticism, autobiographical and other novels. *Cf.* Pierre Cachia, *Ṭāhā Ḥusayn. His Place in the Egyptian Literary Renaissance*. London, 1956.

[85] *Kān mā kān* (Once Upon a Time), p. 121.

[86] *Kān mā kān* (Once Upon a Time), p. 122.

[87] *Kān mā kān* (Once Upon a Time), p. 123.

[88] *Kān mā kān* (Once Upon a Time), p. 43.

[89] *Kān mā kān* (Once Upon a Time), p. 43.

[90] *Kān mā kān* (Once Upon a Time), p. 43.

[91] *Kān mā kān* (Once Upon a Time), p. 43.

[92] *Kān mā kān* (Once Upon a Time), p. 43.

[93] *Kān mā kān* (Once Upon a Time), p. 44.

think that it was *burying* his hopes" [94]. The midwife "would rather *die*" [95] than tell the shaykh that another girl had been born. The shaykh himself is portrayed as ready to kill before he is informed of the sex of the newly born child : "If it is a girl? 'I will strangle her' " [96].

The iron-monger in "A nail-paring" tells how his father used to be a very intemperate man, as far as his parings were concerned, and that he himself had the same character. The outburst at the end of the story, therefore, is hardly a surprise [97].

Nu'aymah has a tendency to account for everything that happens in his stories. Nothing takes place without a perhaps over-explicit preparation. In some stories this has led to curious consequences. The shepherd ("al-Bankārūliyā" = The Baccalaureate) [98] e.g. gathers a handful of the excrements of his sheep after he has sold the herd to finance his son's studies in America. Eight years later, the son, who has finished his studies and who has earned his living for a few years, finds himself out of a job. The father meets his request for financial support with part of the eight year old dung, the rest of the excrement is plastered over the baccalaureate diploma.

Nu'aymah's stories frequently end with a short or long epilogue, which sometimes merely winds up the story, but in other cases seems intended to prick the reader's conscience or to provoke him to some reaction. A story such as "al-'Āqir" (The Barren One) [99] ends in this winding up way : "Somebody from the village of 'Azīz al-Kirbāğ' (= whip) told me that he had seen him in New York recently..." [100]. "Sanatuhā al-ğadīdah" (Her New Year) has a double ending, after having started with a double beginning. The first beginning assesses the fame of the village Yarbūb, depending not in the least on its Shaykh. The second beginning leads to the story of the Shaykh's murder of his newly born daughter, which fact, however, is not explicitly told. The first ending is a kind of epilogue, which tells that the people wish one another a Happy New Year, but that "on the grave-yard behind the church, the trees were moaning, the wind wailing and heaven weeping frozen tears, and the churchbell calling 'A Year of Good Health to You' ". The second ending relates that the village is still famous, and that a gossiping tongue says that the Shaykh has killed his daughter, and that he has stayed out of church since that night. To this the provocative sentence is added "Indeed, the village Yarbūb is

[94] *Kān mā kān* (Once Upon a Time), p. 49.
[95] *Kān mā kān* (Once Upon a Time), p. 45.
[96] *Kān mā kān* (Once Upon a Time), p. 50.
[97] *Cf.* p. 98.
[98] *Abū Baṭṭah* (The Fat-Calved Man), p. 71-78.
[99] *Kān mā kān* (Once Upon a Time), p. 52-83.
[100] *Kān mā kān* (Once Upon a Time), p. 83.

famous for many things!". Much simpler but equally provocative in its ending is the story "Shahīdat al-Shuhd" (The Martyr of the Honey) [101]. The story does not tell that a girl died from bee stings, but that the mother, who had terrorized the girl and who had ordered her to fetch some honey for her sick brother on pain of suffering another harsh punishment, nine years after, kept talking about the self-sacrificing deed of her daughter.

In many of his stories Nu'aymah has tried to establish inner verisimilitude by asserting their historical relevance. He employed to this end one of the commonest devices of having an eye-witness tell what he saw or experienced himself. Sometimes such a narrator is introduced with a few words, as for example, "I met so-and-so who told me", or "We met so-and-so who told us". Such a statement evidently serves the author in that he can disclaim that he invented the story, and the use of the plural "we met" provides the extra certainty of an independent witness. Sometimes the device is made more intricate by the introduction of more than one narrator who passes the story on to another. "'Ulbat Kabrīt" (A Box of matches) [102] and "Hadiyyat al-Ḥayzabūn" (Hayzabun's Present) [103] each have two consecutive narrators, apart from the "I"-narrator. "Sā'at al-kūkū" (The Cuckoo clock) [104] likewise has three : The first narrator tells a story to a man, who in his turn writes it down in a letter which he sends to the narrator who says : "The most precious presents are those which come from unknown givers. I have a letter in my bag...".

It is not without interest to see how such a series of narrators is handled by Nu'aymah. They all vouch for the historical truth of what they are telling, but the variation is such that a cumulative effect is achieved. "Sā'at al-kūkū" (The Cuckoo clock) opens with a narrator telling that he has received a letter dated beginning May 1922, and that it comes from a small Lebanese village as he can read from the postmark. The sender of the letter describes the burial of an emigrant who had returned to Lebanon two years earlier. The author of the letter asserts the truth of what he wrote on a minor point, namely that everybody in the village wept over the grave. He implores the addressee to believe this as he is neither an author nor a poet. His informer, however, begins the story with a fairy-tale opening "Once upon a time" which is also the title of the collection in which the story eventually found a place. Only when he has arrived at the end of the story this last narrator reveals the identity of the main character as his own.

---

101 *Abū Baṭṭah* (The Fat-Calved Man), p. 70.

102 *Akābir* (Notables), p. 106-112.

103 *Abū Baṭṭah* (The Fat-Calved Man), p. 165-173.

104 *Kān mā kān* (Once Upon a Time), p. 7-38.

More subtle in its mixture of historical truth and fairy-tale motifs is "Hadiyyat al-Ḥayzabūn" (Hayzabun's present) [105]. An old lady, reputed for her trustworthiness, poise and fidelity, tells in a tall story contest the strangest event which ever befell her. Her story of the pot with gold, the North African magician and the slaughtered child, however, happened long ago and in a far-away village. The complete manuscript device which has been used in a story such as "Sā'at al-kūkū" (The Cuckoo clock), has been used also in *Mudhakkarāt al-Arqash* in which the Memoirs of Pitted Face form the mainstay, and in *The Book of Mirdad* which contains the discussions and acts of a heavenly messenger noted down by one of his disciples.

The language used in Nu'aymah's writings is a modern variant of the classical Arabic language. Rhymed prose phrases, still popular in the first decades of the twentieth century, are almost absent as are other archaisms. The colloquial language is limited to isolated words. This, however, has not always been the case. In the original versions of the early stories, as far as can be established, Nu'aymah made use of colloquial language for the dialogues in the same way as Haykal did in his *Zaynab*. Nu'aymah, however, limited the use of the colloquial to illiterate persons, whereas literate persons were given the speech of literary language, regardless of their interlocutors. The hybrid character of this solution may have caused Nu'aymah to rephrase the dialect clauses in a language more consistent with that of the other parts of the stories. The play *al-Ābā' wa al-banūn* [106] (Fathers and Sons) escaped this fate, and the introduction in which Nu'aymah discusses the problems and adduces arguments for his option, has remained unchanged. Nu'aymah's knowledge of, and admiration for, Russian literature until 1912 may have influenced him in his choice of a common and simple language.

---

105 *Abū Baṭṭah* (The Fat-Calved Man), p. 165-173.

106 See p. 50, note 14.

V. THE BIOGRAPHY OF ǦIBRĀN AND NU'AYMAH'S AUTOBIOGRAPHY

Biography has always had a fair share of attention in Arabic literature [1]. Its first subject was and still is the Prophet [2], whose sayings and doings soon acquired exemplary value in cases where the Quran did not provide the necessary guidance. Most probably during the Prophet's lifetime already the quest for his pronouncements and for eyewitness accounts of his practice commenced. This knowledge was hoarded in small private collections first, and then found its way into the larger, more or less systematized, collections of tradition literature on the one hand, and into the biography of the Prophet on the other. Ibn Isḥāq's (d. 768) *Sīrat rasūl Allāh* (Life of the Messenger of God), handed down to us through Ibn Hishām's (d. 834) recension is the oldest extant biography of the Prophet [3].

The roots of this biography seem to stretch out into Christian hagiography, in so far as the future role of the Prophet is ominously presaged both before and after his birth and during the years before he was called to Prophethood. Accounts of the warring enterprises of the first Muslims, as recorded by Ibn Isḥāq, remind us of the pre-Islamic *Ayyām al-'Arab* (The Days of the Arabs) [4], which celebrate the raids waged by tribal ancestors.

The biography of the Prophet opened the way for other people to be eternalized through the recordings of their lives. The first Muslim ruler to find a biographer was Maḥmūd, the ruler of Ghaznah from 999-1030, whose 'life' was written by

---

1 On Arabic biography and autobiography *cf.* M. Z. Siddiqi, "The Glory of Arabic Literature. On Literary Biography". *Proceedings 8th All-India Oriental Conference*, 1935, p. 187-286. H. Gottschalk, "Abū 'Ubaid al-Qāsim b.Sallām", "Studie zur Geschichte der arabischen Biographie". *Der Islam* (1936), 23, 245-289. Fr. Rosenthal, "Die arabische Autobiographie" in Studia Arabica I, *Analecta Orientalia*, 14 (1937), 1-40. Georg Misch, *Geschichte der Autobiographie*. Band II, 1, p. 179-303 (Frankfurt am Main, 1955) : Die Selbstdarstellung des arabischen Helden in der vorislamischen Dichtung; Band III, 2, p. 905-1076, (Frankfurt am Main, 1962) : Selbstdarstellungen von Trägern des geistigen Lebens in dem Mittelalterlichen Kulturbereich des Islam. Iḥsān 'Abbās, *Fann al-sīrah* (The Art of Biography), Beirut, Dār al-Thaqāfah, n.d.[2].

2 Cf. A. Wessels, *A Modern Arabic Biography of Muḥammad, A Critical Study of Muḥammad Ḥusayn Ḥaykal's Ḥayāt Muḥammad.* Leiden, 1972.

3 A text-edition was published by Ferd. Wüstenfeld, *Ibn Hišām, Das Leben Muhammed's nach Muhammed Ibn Ishaq.* Göttingen, 1858-60. Translations were published by Gustav Weil. Stuttgart, 1864 and by A. Guillaume, *The Life of Muhammed.* London, O.U.P., 1955.

4 On the *Ayyām al-'arab* see W. Gaskel, "Aijam al-'Arab. Studien zur altarabischen Epik". Supplementum Voluminis. *Islamica* III, fasc. 5, 1931, 1-99.

al-ʿUtbī in his *al-Kitāb al-Yamīnī* or "the Book of Yamīn al-Dawlah Maḥmūd al-Ghaznāwī" [5]. The legendary Saladin had biographers in ʿImad al-Dīn al-Kātib al-Iṣfahānī (1125-1201) and in Bahā' al-Dīn Ibn Shaddād (1145-1234) [6].

The normal course for the biographer was to emphasize the greatness of his subject, and to enlarge upon the deeds which contributed to that greatness. A notable exception to this rule was Ibn Mammātī (1209), who satirized the maladministration of Qaraqush, one of the Ministers of Saladin, in his *Kitāb al-Fāshūsh fī aḥkām Qaraqūsh* (The book of feeblemindedness in the ordinances of Qaraqūsh) [7]. His example, however, seems not to have been followed. Another kind of biographical literature, the hagiographic *Vitae*, thrived within the Christian Arabic communities. Graf's *Geschichte der christlichen arabischen Literatur* [8] is a witness to the popularity of this *genre*.

Of more modern times is the biography of Muḥammad ʿAbduh (1905) by his pupil Rashīd Riḍā, first in the latter's magazine *al-Manār* (The Lighthouse) [9], and later in a two-volumed book, *Ta'rīkh al-Ustādh al-Imām al-Shaykh Muḥammad ʿAbduh* [10]. These biographies are also one-sided, in that they have an eye for ʿAbduh's greatness alone, but an effort is made to probe into the personality beyond the immediate surface.

Apart from the full-fledged biography stand works containing short biographical notes about great numbers of people. These works were originally conceived as auxiliaries to the tradition literature, in which each bit of tradition was supported by a chain of transmitters. Only when the trustworthiness of each of the transmitters and the reliability of the chain they formed was beyond doubt was the tradition labelled 'sound'. It was therefore imperative to know these men, and this led to what was later called the *ʿilm al-riǧāl* (knowledge of the men). In the beginning the individual collector of traditions kept records of his intellectual ancestors. These small lists

---

5 An English translation was prepared by J. Reynolds, *The Kitab-i-Yamini. Historical Memoirs of the Amír Sabaktagín, and the Sultán Mahmúd of Ghazna, Early Conquerors of Hindustan, and Founders of the Ghaznavide Dynasty. Translated from the Persian Version of the Contemporary Arabic Chronicle of al-Utbi.* London, 1858.

6 Critical edition of ʿImād al-Dīn al-Kātib al-Iṣfahānī, *Kitāb al-fatḥ al-qussī fī l-fatḥ al-qudsī* by Comte Carlo de Landberg. Leiden, E. J. Brill, 1888. On the basis of the two biographies Sir Hamilton Gibb wrote his *The Life of Saladin. From the works of ʿImād ad-Dīn and Bahā' ad-Dīn.* Oxford, At the Clarendon Press, 1973.

7 Edited by P. Casanova, *Qarakouch, sa légende et son histoire.* Le Caire, 1892.

8 G. Graf, *Geschichte der christlichen arabischen Literatur.* 5 Vols. Città del Vaticano, 1944-1953.

9 The biography was published in *al-Manār*, Vol. VIII (1315H = 1905/6) fasc. 10, 11, 12, 13, 14 and 23.

10 Cairo, 1931.

were compiled into biographical dictionaries by men like Ibn Sa'd in his *Kitāb al-ṭabaqāt al-kabīr* (The Great Book of Generations, i.e. first the generation of the Prophet, then the generation of the so-called 'followers', and then that of the 'followers of the followers') [11]. Subsequent collections developed great variety, both in the arrangement of the material and in their purpose. The works could be arranged alphabetically, chronologically or according to local deliminations, with or without subdivisions. Some collections, as the histories of various cities, restricted themselves to men of local significance, other works concerned the learned, the poets, the judges, the ministers, or they recorded the history of a dynasty. Moreover the entries could vary between a somewhat extensive biography and the simple recording of the names and dates of death. It is possible that the first autobiographies were composed by the compilers of biographical collections and added to their books. Others will have given their *curricula vitae* on request to the compilers of what may be called the forerunners of the *Who's Who* [12].

One of the first autobiographical works in Arab literary history is al-Ghazzālī's (d. 1111) *al-Munqidh min al-ḍalāl* (What rescues (or 'rescued') from error) [13], which could be called an *apologia pro vita sua.* The frequently mentioned autobiography of 'Usāmah b. Munqidh (d. Damascus 1188) is a collection of loosely connected anecdotes, and should more properly be named 'Memoirs', as was done by Philip Hitti in his translation of the work [14]. More like an autobiography is Ibn Khaldūn's (d. 1406) *al-Ta'rīf bi Ibn Khaldūn wa riḥlatuhu gharban wa sharqan* (Making acquain-

---

[11] Otto Loth, *Das Classenbuch des Ibn Sa'd. Einleitende Untersuchungen über Authentie und Inhalt nach den handschriftlichen Überresten.* Leipzig, J.C. Hinrichs, 1869. Otto Loth, "Ursprung und Bedeutung der Ṭabaḳât, vornehmlich der des Ibn Sa'd". *ZDMG* xxiii (1869), 593-614. A critical edition was made under the directorship of E. Sachau. 8 vols. Leiden, 1904-1917. Three volumes of indices were published in 1921, 1928 and 1940 respectively.

[12] See Fr. Rosenthal, "Die arabische Autobiographie" in "Studia Arabica I", *Analecta Orientalia,* 14 (1937), p. 19.

[13] Translations were published by J. H. Kramers, *Al-Ghazzali. De redder uit de dwaling.* Amsterdam, de Arbeiderspers, 1951. W. Montgomery Watt, *The Faith and Practice of al-Ghazali.* London, George Allen and Unwin Ltd, 1953. 2nd. impr. 1963.

[14] Hartwig Derenbourg, *Ousâmâ ibn Mounkidh. Un émir syrien au premier siècle des Croisades (1095-1188).* Deuxième partie : *Texte arabe de l'autobiographie d'Ousâma.* Paris, 1886, A translation was published by Derenbourg with the title : *Souvenirs historiques et récits de chasse par un émir syrien du douzième siècle. Autobiographie d'Ousâma ibn Mounkidh intitulée l'Instruction par les exemples.* Paris, Ernest Leroux, 1895. G. R. Potter, *The Autobiography of Ousâma,* London, 1929, is a translation of Derenbourg's French version. Philip K. Hitti, *An Arab-Syrian Gentleman and Warrior in the Period of the Crusades. Memoirs of Usâma Ibn Munqidh.* (Kitāb al-i'tibār) New York, 1929. This book was republished by Khayats, Beirut, 1964 : Philip K. Hitti, *Memoirs of an Arab-Syrian Gentleman or an Arab Knight in the Crusades. Memoirs of Usāmah Ibn Munqidh.* (Kitāb al-i'tibār).

tance with Ibn Khaldūn and his travels west and east), which he appended to his *Kitāb al-'Ibar* (World History)[15].

Fāris ibn al-Shidyāq's *al-Sāq 'alā al-sāq fī mā huwa al-Fāryāq*[16] is not an autobiography in the strictest sense, but it contains enough elements to consider it the first Arabic autobiography in modern times.

More recently Ṭāhā Ḥusayn wrote his autobiographical novel in three parts, the first part of which dates back to 1926[17]. Another name to be mentioned here is Salāmah Mūsā, whose *Tarbiyat Salāmah Mūsā* was first published in 1947[18]. Aḥmad Amīn's *Ḥayātī* (My Life) came out in 1950.

Nu'aymah's book about Ǧibrān was his first effort in biography[19]. It was written at a time when the so-called *'biographie romancée'* as it flourished under the impact of the works of Maurois, Strachey, Ludwig and Zweig, was a literary issue of some importance[20]. It seems probable that Nu'aymah knew of these developments and tried to take heed of them. One of the outcomes of his contact with the modern biography seems to be the more or less independent point of view he adopts with regard to his subject. Instead of writing one long eulogy, Nu'aymah shows the shortcomings of his 'hero'.

---

15 A text-edition of this biography was made by Muḥammad Ibn Tāwīt al-Ṭanǧī (Cairo, 1951) and reproduced without the critical apparatus, but with the other footnotes in the Beirut edition of the *Kitāb al-'ibar*, Beirut, 1966-1968, Vol. VIII, 795-1224.

16 See Iḥsān 'Abbās, *Fann al-sīrah* (The Art of Biography), Beirut, n.d.², p. 141. Cf. also Ch. I, p. 13.

17 The first two parts of Ṭāhā Ḥuseyn's autobiography were published in the form of a novel with the title *al-Ayyām* (The Days), in 1926 and 1939 respectively. The first volume was translated and published with the title *An Egyptian Childhood*, London, 1932. The second volume was translated into English and published with the title *The Stream of the Days*, Cairo, 1943. A revised edition of this last book was published in London, 1948. *Mudhakkarāt Ṭāhā Ḥusayn*, Beirut, 1967, continues the autobiography begun in *al-Ayyām*. *Cf.* "The Memoirs of Taha Husayn" by M. Perlmann, *Bibliotheca Orientalis* XXX (1973), 13-15. *Mudhakkarāt Ṭ. Ḥ.* has also been published in Cairo, 1972, with the title *al-Ayyām*, part three.

18 Salāmah Mūsā, *Tarbiyat Salāmah Mūsā*. First edition, Cairo, 1947; second edition, Cairo, 1958. An English translation by L. O. Schuman was published in Leiden, 1961, with the title : *The Education of Salama Musa.*

19 Mīkhā'īl Nu'aymah, *Ǧibrān Khalīl Ǧibrān. Ḥayātuhu, mawtuhu, adabuhu, fannuhu* (Ǧibrān Khalīl Ǧibrān, His life, his death, his literature, his art). Beirut, 1934. Page numbers mentioned in the footnotes refer to the fourth edition, Beirut, 1960.

20 Cf. S. Dresden, *De Structuur van de Biografie*. Den Haag, 1956. Other works consulted for introductory purposes are : Jan Romein, *De Biografie. Een Inleiding*. Amsterdam, 1946. A. Chorus, *Het Beeld van de Mens in de Oude Biographie en Hagiographie*. Den Haag, 1962. A. Chorus, *Vormen van Zelfkennis*. Den Haag, 1966.

The picture of Ğibrān that is gained from Nu'aymah's description is that of a somewhat infantile man, quickly offended and easily flattered, ponderous, loquacious, sensual and moralistic, seeking literary and artistic recognition. Sometimes the author's descriptions of Ğibrān's weaker sides are not without overemphasis. His search for recognition becomes : "his soul, so hungry for 'greatness and glory' " [21], or "his heart ever hungry for 'greatness and glory' " [22] and again "the 'greatness and glory' [23] which he thought were his due". Nu'aymah shows himself offended when he relates that Ğibrān once mentioned Bombay as his birthplace : "It became a source of shame for him to own as his birthplace an obscure village like Bisharrī, and as his country, a small country like Lebanon. A man like him, he became convinced, must have a mystic birth in a mystic birthplace" [24]. Nu'aymah is also not very appreciative of Ğibrān's love-life to which he devotes considerable attention. Especially this information was subjected to severe criticism. The issue, however, was not so much whether Nu'aymah's disclosures were based on facts or not. The first protesters argued that such things ought not to be made public. To Amīn al-Rayḥānī [25] the biography constituted nothing less than a breach of faith, and the American poetess and friend of Ğibrān in his last years, Barbara Young, singled Nu'aymah out as "One, who shall be nameless, has departed from the faith. The others continue with the same devotion and loyalty to their noble inheritance and to the memory of their beloved friend..." [26]. Al-Rayḥānī was more explicit in his criticism, which he formulated in a few pertinent questions : "Is it allowed for me to spy upon the heart of somebody whose friendship to me is sincere, and that I divulge what he opened up to me in moments of despair or when his soul was blended with mine as water and wine?" [27] Another question of al-Rayḥānī pinpoints the trustworthiness of the present biography : "Who told you what Ğibrān said in his heart? ... when there was deep in him a question he dared not to reveal, even not to himself, as you say, how did he disclose it to you or to anybody else?" [28].

---

[21] English ed. p. 137, Arabic ed. 143. All quotations have been taken from the English edition.

[22] English ed. p. 140, Arabic ed. p. 145.

[23] English ed. p. 179. The Arabic version reads here : "to obtain from the two (his art and his literature) the share he thought his due", p. 182.

[24] English ed. p. 129, Arabic ed. p. 134.

[25] Amīn al-Rayḥānī wrote an open letter in the Beirut newspaper *al-Bilād* of January 6, 1934. This letter has been quoted in full in *Sab'ūn* III, 104-107. It has been included in the *Rasā'il Amīn al-Rayḥānī, 1896-1940* (The Letters of Amīn al-Rayḥānī), Beirut, 1959, p. 439-443. Another early criticism came from Īlīyā Abū Māḍī, "Ğibrān taḥt mabādi' Nu'aymah" (Ğibrān according to the Principles of Nu'aymah) — *al-Samīr*, no. 18, New York, 1935.

[26] Barbara Young, *This Man from Lebanon.* New York, 1945, 14th print, New York, 1967, p. 34.

[27] *Rasā'il Amīn al-Rayḥānī*, p. 441, *Sab'ūn* III, 105.

[28] *Rasā'il Amīn al-Rayḥānī*, p. 440, *Sab'ūn* III, 105.

Later attacks against Nuʿaymah's biography of Ǧibrān concentrated on its factualness, but these attacks have lost much of their vigour after the discovery of the correspondence between Ǧibrān and his 'guardian angel' Mary Haskell and the latter's diary [29]. The question of this moment is, how well informed was Mary Haskell.

One of the criticisms raised against the biography is that Nuʿaymah is too forcefully present. This refers to the period of Nuʿaymah's acquaintance and friendship with Ǧibrān. The life of Ǧibrān before his meeting with Nuʿaymah is related in the form of a novella, not unlike the above-mentioned *biographie romancée*. The period after their meeting is covered by some memoirs of Nuʿaymah and by discussions of Ǧibran's work in those years, the whole amounting to a critique of the man and his work [30]. The presence of Nuʿaymah is most acutely felt in his assessment of the Nietzschean period of Ǧibrān, which started, according to the biography, in the fall of 1912 [31]. The chapter "The Grave-digger" [32] contains some four pages of quotations from *Thus Spoke Zarathustra* which are preceded by a summary of the teachings of Zarathustra as understood by Nuʿaymah : "There is no God but me. I am the creator and the creation. I am the goal and the way to the goal. I shall carry man beyond man ..." [33]. A better interpretation of these teachings is given by Nuʿaymah in the Foreword to the collected Arabic works of Ǧibrān *al-Maǧmuʿah al-kāmilah li-muʾallafāt Ǧibrān Khalīl Ǧibrān* : "Ǧibrān revolted with Nietzsche not only against the rulers and the monks, but against all and sundry and against their traditions, their yardsticks, their scales and against the cracking foundations on which they erected the castle of their lives. Their beliefs, politics or philosophies did not set them free of fear, humiliation, slavery and poverty. On the contrary, it strengthened in their souls fears and vices without numbers as it killed in them the creative will which

[29] The first publication on the letters in Arabic came from Tawfīq Ṣāyigh, "Ǧibrān wa Mary Haskell, qiṣṣat ʿalāqah" (Ǧibrān and Mary Haskell, The Story of a Relation), *Ḥiwār* 22, May-June 1966, p. 5-48. Idem, "Aḍwāʾ ʿalā Ǧibrān. Ḥayātuhu al-thaqāfiyyah" (Light on Ǧibrān, His cultural life). *Ḥiwār* 23, July-August 1966, Beirut, p. 5-43. A selection of the letters was published by Virginia Hilu, *Beloved Prophet. The Love Letters of Kahlil Gibran and Mary Haskell and her private journal.* London, 1972.

[30] The novella-like part stretches from p. 13-108 and p. 119-129 (Arabic edition p. 22-114 and p. 124-135). The period of Nuʿaymah's acquaintance with Ǧibrān until the latter's death fills the pages 3-12 and 130-232 (Arabic edition p. 13-21 and p. 136-243). The gap between p. 108 and 119 (Arabic edition p. 117-123) results from the inclusion of an allegory about the sale of the isle of Manhattan by the Red Indians.

[31] English version p. 108 and 119, Arabic ed. p. 114 and 124. Cf. S. Wild, "Friedrich Nietzsche and Gibran Kahlil Gibran". *Al-Abḥāth* 22, nr. 3-4 (December 1969), p. 47-57.

[32] English version p. 119-129, Arabic ed. p. 124-135. In this chapter Nuʿaymah deals with Ǧibrān's story "Haffār al-qubūr" (The Gravedigger) in *al-ʿAwāṣif* (Tempests) : *Al-Maǧmūʿah al-kāmilah li-muʾallafāt Ǧibrān Khalīl Ǧibrān al-ʿarabiyyah* (The Complete Arabic Works of Ǧibrān Khalīl Ǧibrān), Beirut, 1964, p. 367-371.

[33] English version p. 119, Arabic ed. p. 125.

alone is the guarantee that it will make them reach the ideal man, or the genius, or the superman"[34]. Nu'aymah makes it quite clear that he abhors Nietzsche, and that he resents Ğibrān's enthusiasm for *Thus Spoke Zarathustra.* This aversion, together with his own optimistic philosophy, may have led Nu'aymah to identify anything pessimistic in Ğibrān's writings of that period as Nietzschean[35]. It is equally possible that Ğibrān himself was of the same opinion, and in fact suggested it to Nu'aymah. Anyhow, Ğibrān's gravedigger is at a far remove from Nietzsche's Zarathustra. Ğibrān's hero is instructed by a supernatural being[36], whereas Zarathustra follows his own judgement. Zarathustra has a message for mankind about the coming of the Superman, but Ğibrān's man has an occupation not catered for by Zarathustra, digging graves for a mankind already dead from its birth. Lastly, in Ğibrān's work reality is not something to be found in this world, which contrasts sharply with Nietzsche's call to remain true to the earth.

Though Nu'aymah appears not to see the fundamental difference between Ğibrān's gravedigger and Nietzsche's Zarathustra, he is aware of some inconsistency in Ğibrān's partisanship for Nietzsche. After having said that Nietzsche's temper, will and faith were not Ğibrān's Nu'aymah continues : "The kinship he found between himself and the German iconoclast did not reach beyond the fact that both had inordinate imaginations which refused to be clothed in commonplace words and colours. Otherwise their worlds were far apart. But Nietzsche's first impact on Ğibrān was so strong that it carried him off his feet and almost uprooted him from his Oriental soil, leaving him much embittered against the world"[37].
At the end of his discussions of the Gravedigger Nu'aymah adduces another reason for Ğibrān's bitterness, which does not seem to be far from the mark : "His war against conventions was a war for recognition. If men would only accept him as he accepted himself, he would willingly condone their frailties. The bitterness the fight engendered in his heart was the bitterness of the warrior unable to wring a word of praise or submission from his opponent. It was quite different from Nietzsche's bitterness"[38].

An uncommon feature of this biography is that it has a leading thought, or as Nadeem Naimy writes : "the preconceived intention of unfolding the various stages of his man-God pilgrimage". Naimy, therefore, likens the biography to Bunyan's *Pilgrim's*

---

[34] First edition of *al-Mağmū'ah al-kāmilah*, Beirut, 1964, p. 25.

[35] Cf. English ed. p. 142, Arabic ed. p. 147.

[36] In "The Gravedigger" the hero is ordered to divorce his wife and to marry the daughter of a *ğinn*, because only the *ğinns* represent reality : who does not belong to their world belongs to the sphere of 'doubt and confusion'. *al-Mağmū'ah al-kāmilah* p. 369.

[37] English ed. p. 142, Arabic ed. p. 147.

[38] English ed. p. 129, Arabic ed. p. 135. The English text is milder than the Arabic.

Progress [39]. The theme of the book is indicated in the question Nu'aymah asks himself when sitting at Ǧibrān's death-bed in a New York hospital : "What food have you stored, my brother, for this journey?" [40]. The labels affixed to the three periods which Nu'aymah discerns in Ǧibrān's life are meant to indicate what spiritual headway was made. These titles : Twilight, Night, and Dawn, were impressive enough to be taken over by Kh. Hawi in his *Kahlil Gibran. His Background, Character and Works* [41].

As far as stylistics are concerned, the book is not a model of unity. The opening chapter about Ǧibrān's last hours in a New York hospital followed by the chapters on his life ever under the spectre of death seem to be an excellent concept for a biography. The unity is broken by the different treatment of the periods before and after Nu'aymah's acquaintance with Ǧibrān. Towards the end of the first period another cleavage occurs caused by the insertion of an alien element, which is an allegory about materialism, personified as the Great Penny, getting hold of Manhattan and thereby of America [42]. This disharmony, however, should not obscure the fact that this book constituted a new experience in Arabic biography.

Nu'aymah's autobiography *Sab'ūn* (Seventy) is one of his most important works. It covers his life almost from the cradle to his seventieth year. The first edition was published in 1959/60 in three stout volumes. Each of them deals with a well-defined period of Nu'aymah's life. The first volume informs the reader of Nu'aymah's early childhood, his schooling in Biskintā, Nazareth and Poltava (Ukraine) and ends with his departure for the U.S.A. in 1911. Volume II covers the entire period of his study and work in the U.S.A., and volume III concerns the period beginning with Nu'aymah's return to Lebanon in April 1932. To tell the story of his life Nu'aymah has not limited himself to one literary technique : anecdotes, stories, descriptions, sermons and biographical notes of others are all there [43].

The first volume opens with a charming story which gives an excellent characterization of the *milieu* into which Nu'aymah was born. The story tells of little Mīkhā'īl's bewilderment over having to pray to his Father in Heaven to turn the dust in the

---

39 Nadeem N. Naimy, *Mikhail Naimy. An Introduction.* Originally written as a Ph. D. thesis, Cambridge, it was published in 1967 by the American University of Beirut.

40 English ed. p. 10, Arabic ed. p. 20.

41 Khalil S. Hawi, *Kahlil Gibran. His Background, Character and Works.* Beirut, 1953.

42 See footnote 30.

43 For referential purposes the following editions have been used : Volume I, 2nd edition, Beirut, 1962; Volume II, 2nd edition, Beirut, 1964; Volume III, 1st edition, Beirut, 1960. Cf. Francesco Gabrieli, l'Autobiografia di Mikhail Nu'aima, *Oriente Moderno* XLIX, n. 6-7 (Giogno-Luglio, 1969), p. 381-387.

hands of his father in America into gold. This story is followed by a description of the members of the family and especially of the mother, who was the driving force behind all the enterprises of the male members of the family. Her energy and ambition are appreciated and mildly criticised in a passage which begins with her father's opinion : "He used to say to my mother whenever an occasion presented itself : 'You are the sister of men. O, lucky the hour in which you came to us. Without you my house would be in ruins!' He was right in what he said. My mother had a great deal of inborn sagacity, acute sensitivity, good taste and foresight in the management of the house and the rearing of her children. But her ambition to better her position did not know of boundaries" [44].

The description of the family is followed by that of the house inclusive of the materials of which it was built and the conveniences and inconveniences appertaining to it. Then the scene is widened to the village. At this stage the reader is almost casually drawn into a conversation with the author : "The reader may forgive me when I stop a while to describe to him that house, which is but an example of thousands of village dwellings spread over the higher slopes of the Lebanese mountain" [45]. Then he introduces the reader into the house and shows him around and finally answers the questions laid into the mouth of the reader. Likewise Nu'aymah describes al-Shakhrūb, five kilometers from Biskintā, where the family cultivated some land during summer. But this time the description betrays Nu'aymah's emotional attachment to the spot : "What use is it to you when I say that al-Shakhrūb is a small patch of land on the slope of mount Ṣannīn, with plenty of rocks, trees, thistles and birds, when you have not dwelt as I did, with those rocks, trees, thistles and birds? when you have not known, as I did, that they all bustle with life and movement, day and night? and when you have not seen it, as I did, at daybreak, in the heat of noon, at dawn and in the light of the stars and the moon? You have not seen the pecker climbing the sides of the trees with its sharp talons. You have not heard it sing its sublime songs when it had begun to climb. You have not ..." [46].

Other chapters deal with Mīkhā'īl entering school, the return of his father from America, the foundation of an elementary school by the "Imperial Orthodox Palestine Society", called shortly thereafter the "Russian School", and Nu'aymah's qualification for further study at the Russian school in Nazareth at the age of twelve. The quest for a birthday certificate to obtain an identity-card has been recorded in the form of a discussion with the village priest : "I need a birthday certificate, father".

---

44 *Sab'ūn* I, 11.

45 *Sab'ūn* I, 18.

46 *Sab'ūn* I, 38.

He threw a wondering gaze at me from under his spectacles and said : "A birth-certificate? How should I remember when you were born?".
I said : "Didn't you baptize me?".
He said : "Certainly"
— "Then a certificate of baptism, please".
— "I am not God Almighty my son to remember the date of your baptism".
— "Doesn't the church have records?"
— "What kind of records? We baptize who is born, we bury who has died, we marry who wants to marry. Why records? What is their use?".
— "But I have to travel. I must have a birth-certificate. What to do?"
— "Go to your mother, or father, or grandfather. Perhaps they remember when you were born. Go and we will look into the matter of the certificate" [47].

A large part of volume I consists of diary-fragments which Nuʿaymah had written down during his stay in Poltava, Ukraine. Thanks to this written material the author has been able to give an extensive coverage of his stay in Russia and thus to highlight one of the crucial periods in his intellectual development. He keeps silent, however, about the kind of instruction he received during those years, Russian literature being a notable exception. Much of the last subject, moreover, seemed to have been learned outside class, and Nuʿaymah tells us that he and his friends were discussing literature with one of the teachers or among themselves, but not what and how they were discussing it. In some of the entries of the diary, but also in the chapters following the completion of his studies in Nazareth and immediately after his stay in Poltava, the author proceeds to a stock-taking of his religious beliefs and of his aspirations in life [48].

One of the stylistic devices Nuʿaymah is using to translate an emotion is enumeration in more or less the same manner as has been observed in his poetry. Turning himself against the very act of bewailing the dead he enumerates what mourners do to express their grief : "Had I not heard them repeat at various occasions : "We all are the harvest of death", "God is the One Remaining", "Death is a grace", "Death is true"? As long as they know that all life belongs to death and that nobody remains but God and that death is true, why do they — every time one of their living has died — loosen the hair, beat the cheeks, tear the clothes, shed tears, wail, moan, abuse, then conclude with wrapping their body and their hearts in black, so that no smile slips from them, no glass is clinked in their houses, no song but those of lament and distress are heard?

---

47 *Sabʿūn* I, 104.

48 The chapters referred to are : "bayna ʿālamayn" (Between two worlds), *Sabʿūn* I, p. 156-167, espec. p. 157-159, and "ʿabra al-muḥīṭ" (Across the ocean), *Sabʿūn* I, p. 273-283, espec. p. 284-289.

Look at my mother. But it is as if she is not my mother after the news of her brother's death has reached her. Where is her even, elegant, proud gait? She walks as somebody carrying the burdens of heaven and earth on his back. Where are her wide, intelligent and dreamy eyes? They are ponds of blood, and their lashes are wounded by tears. Where is that tender red flush diffused over her wheat-coloured face? It has turned into an ashen paleness as covers the face of the chronic diseased. Where is the haughtiness of her nose gently curved near its tip? That nose is now the mark of humbleness and brokenness. Where is the sweetness of her clear, loving voice? It is a hoarse, wheezy voice. I do not remember that I was distressed by the death of my uncle. I do recall that I wept for the weeping of my mother and that I was distressed by her appearance" [49]. The first half of this fragment shows the heaping of verbs. It ends in a longer sentence with three subordinate clauses. The second half consists of rhetorical questions each containing a noun defined by up to three adjectives. The question is followed each time by a clause. Together they tell that his mother's grief affected her gait, eyes, face, nose, and eyes, which again is an enumeration. Especially this second half has the force of a lamentation, but it is a living person that is the object of the dirge.

More joyful but equally rhetorical are the lines in which Nu'aymah exults over his going to the land of the Bible, though he does not forget to mention that it will be his first separation from his elderly home : "Where are you, Palestine — O promised land overflowing with milk and honey? Where are you, dream of Moses and captive of Joshua, the son of Nun? O beloved of David and Salomo, O Inspiration of Isaiah and author of the book of Job, O Stage on which the most exalted scenes of life and the acts of the most horrible tragedy since that of Eden followed each other, Where are you O Nazareth of the carpenter Joseph and his bride Maria, the mother of the hero of that life and tragedy? My God, how far away are you O land of milk and honey, how far away is your Nazareth? Is there with you something useful for this youngster, who has not yet completed his thirteenth year, is there with you something that will replace the humble nest, the family and his al-Shakhrūb" [50].

The diary fragments are stylistically not very different from the other parts of the book, although there are almost fifty years between them. It is, however, clearly discernible that the diary was written by a young man. For instance the description of Safka, the attendant of the Seminary in Poltava, is direct and without a shade of grey to tone down the black : "O Safka, Safka! I do not know why I do despise you so much. Is it because you threatened me twice "to return me to Palestine" for my absence from church? Or is it it that I consider you devoid of human feelings? Or

[49] *Sab'ūn* I, p. 94-95.

[50] *Sab'ūn* I, p. 103.

is it that you find no nobler and more exalted function in life than to spy upon the students? and then to report them to the board so that they will lower their marks for conduct and that this lowering will end in chasing them from school? How I wanted to love you, but my heart does not obey me. How I wanted to respect you, but I do not know of anything in you worthy of respect" [51].

The second volume deals with Nuʿaymah's study in Seattle, his stay in New York, his military service during the last months of World War I and the foundation, flourishing and end of *al-Rābiṭah al-qalamiyyah* (The Pen League) in New York. The basic material of this volume is provided by the notes he wrote down in France after the war had ended, by letters to and from friends in America and to his brother Nasīb during the latter's study in France until 1931 and by his own poetry and prose-works of this period, as well as those of his friends in the *Rābiṭah*. A very incisive experience was Nuʿaymah's enlistment in the U.S. army and his taking part in the last actions of the war in France. This period of fourteen months until his departure from France in 1919 fills almost one fifth of volume II, which covers twenty years of Nuʿaymah's life [52]. He gives detailed descriptions of the equipment of the individual soldier as well as of the mentality in the army, of life aboard a transport ship and of an army moving to the front-line. The last operations of the war in which Nuʿaymah was actively involved are recorded. The end of this compulsory stay in France comes with four months of study at the University of Rennes.

Arabic literature meant something to Nuʿaymah during his years in the U.S.A., and this left its mark on the second volume of his autobiography. Much space has been given to *al-Rābiṭah al-qalamiyyah* (The Pen League) [53]. The aims of the co-operating authors and poets are explained in one chapter, together with short characterizations of each of them. The work of some of the members of the League is discussed in the chapter "The Dough is Fermenting" [54], whereas the social esteem the group gradually became to enjoy among the rich Arab immigrants forms the backbone of some stories of the chapter "From the Life of the Colony" [55]. The activities of the individual members of the League fill many a line in other chapters whether or not they deal with literary matters. Nuʿaymah's own work is amply represented in this volume. He deals with his own poetry in more than one chapter [56]. One chapter has been

---

51 *Sabʿūn* I, p. 182.
52 *Sabʿūn* II, p. 78-134.
53 *Sabʿūn* II, p. 163-175.
54 *Sabʿūn* II, p. 145-150.
55 *Sabʿūn* II, p. 216-224.
56 The poetry he wrote under the impress of his relation with Bella, "Afāqa 'l-qalb" (The Heart awoke), p. 151-162 and "Ayyuhā 'l-ḥubb" (O, Love), *Sabʿūn* II, p. 181-186. Other poems are quoted in "Thawrah wa Hudnah" (A Rebellion and a Truce), *Sabʿūn* II, p. 196-208 and elsewhere in this second volume of the autobiography.

devoted to *al-Ghirbāl* (The Sieve) [57] and another to the story of the Cuckoo-clock [58], which he had written to make his younger brother Nağīb give up his emigration plans. Many of the writings of this period are referred to or are subject to quotation in the other chapters of the volume.

The political issues of the time, notwithstanding Nu'aymah's active participation in the war effort and his leading role in the secret movement "Free Syria", have been dealt with rather cursorily. The famine in the Lebanese Mountain, after the locust plague in 1915 and the simultaneous sealing off of the area by the Turks, takes up the greater part of the chapter "The World Takes Fire" [59]. His own loyalties he expresses in one sentence : "I kept wishing its (Germany's) breakdown, because it befriended Turkey, the enemy of my country, and because it was the enemy of Russia I was befriended with and which I loved" [60].

The aftermath of the war with regard to the Middle East is dealt with in not more than two and half pages. One of the most far-reaching decisions with regard to the Middle East, the Balfour Declaration, elicited a four-line fierce comment almost without parallel in his other writings : "There was the Balfour Declaration. The Balfour Declaration decreed that a stranger enter a house occupied by its people and that he enter it forcibly and with the armed support of the British sovereign. Then he tells the habitants : "Do not worry. The house will remain yours, but it will be my 'national home', nothing more". That is a promise which even the demons of our lord Salomo cannot give — let alone fulfil" [61].

Throughout this volume Nu'aymah demonstrates a certain fondness for the dialogue and for the monologue, forms he not infrequently uses to pass on some information to the reader. This last aspect seems to dominate the self-interrogation of Nu'aymah, who is thinking of returning to Lebanon : "What binds you still to this terrible whirlpool? Bella? The ties between you and her have gradually vanished. It was necessary for them to dissolve in that way so as not to end into disaster. Bella, today, is a bit of perfume in your life and doubtless you are a bit of perfume in hers. How good it is to leave fragrant remembrances in human souls and to take with you such remembrances from them. But, what are you going to do with the relation that grew of late? What are you going to do with her who took your heart by assault, whose name is Njonja, and you thought your heart unassailable?" [62].

---

57 *Sab'ūn* II, 187-195.

58 *Sab'ūn* II, 233-240, *Kān mā kān*, p. 7-38.

59 *Sab'ūn* II, 35-41.

60 *Sab'ūn* II, 41.

61 *Sab'ūn* II, 133.

62 *Sab'ūn* II, 280.

A rather typical fragment consisting of a number of exclamatory sentences, rhetorical and other questions, and an anticlimax, conveys Nuʿaymah's emotions during a nightly two-hour reconnaissance-duty at the French front-line. His mounting indignation over being involved in the war leads to the exclamation : "Witness, O night. Witness, O stars, that man is baser than the animals; that he who is proud of his brains becomes brainless in the war. He who maims the sound and then tries to revalidate what he mutilated". A three times repeated "Why" and the question "Until when this madness"? end this first outburst. Then Wilson's slogan "Peace without Victory" is mentioned. The statement that the war is drawing to an end evokes a new series of questions about the last bullets and shells, ending again with a three times repeated "Why?". The anticlimax is formed by the exchange of greetings which follows the arrival of Nuʿaymah's relief [63].

Another fragment containing all the ingredients mentioned above describes Nuʿaymah's first serious confrontation with the New York labour market after his demobilization. Sometimes he seems to address the reader directly but at other times the texts seem to be nearer to a *monologue intérieur* : "I had to think about work to earn a living and work in a world which is governed by the law of the jungle does not come to you on a silver tray nor does it search for you. You have to go to it and to look for it. Where should I search and how? There is shyness as well as pride in my character which prevent me from offering myself to others and from speaking about my qualities and capabilities. Who will save me today from this embarrassing situation from which the recommendations of the Russian councillor had saved me when I came to New York three years ago?" A number of questions follows the last of which runs : "Or must I stop in the middle of the road and shout at the top of my voice : "Hey, you people. Mankind. People of God..." The anticlimax, or, perhaps better, the climax, of the story consists of the answer to the question : "Who will save me...", saying that "the hidden hand ... or it might please you to call it 'fate' — saved me this time like it had saved me at previous occasions — without the slightest effort of inquiry from my side" [64]. These emotional parts, to be true, are balanced to an extent by more sober descriptions which fill great portions of the book.

The third volume of Nuʿaymah's autobiography begins with the journey home from New York to Beirut. About the journey itself nothing is said except that he had the sea as a companion for twenty days. His friend, Iskandar al-Yāziǧī, with whom he shared a cabin, is not mentioned in this volume before the second chapter, when they take leave of each other upon their arrival in Beirut. Instead the first chapter is

---

63 *Sabʿūn* II, 116-117.

64 *Sabʿūn* II, 138-139.

one of contemplation about an eternal order governing all being much in the same way as earlier periods of transition had been marked by contemplation.

The impressions of Beirut after twenty years of absence and the cumbersome journey to Biskintā are related in some detail. In the following chapter Nu'aymah describes the reunion with the family. Most of the descriptive passages concern the ups and downs of the family : the digging of a well in Biskintā, the building of a new house, the provision of running water in al-Shakhrūb, the cousins born during Nu'aymah's stay in the U.S.A. and the deaths of his brother Nasīb, his father and his mother before and during World War II.

To his father Nu'aymah devoted the chapter "Bū Dīb takes leave of al-Shakhrūb" [65]. Of particular interest is the fact that there are two strings of narrative in the relevant passage. One string concerns the digging of a tunnel to pipe water to al-Shakhrūb and the other string relates the last stay of his father in al-Shakhrūb. The fragment translated below follows a description of the efforts spent to dig the tunnel and of his father's going to al-Shakhrūb : "... How often I saw him sitting under his beloved oak-tree, his hands on his stick, his chin on his hands, his eyes wandering from summit to summit, from wadi to wadi, from field to field, as if he wandered through the leaves of a dear book which he knew by heart".

"I once approached him when he was in that state and I asked him : About what are you thinking, father? and he answered : I am thinking of mankind, my son, how they are born, live and die. Don't you agree with me that people are born near-dead? Then they gradually arise from death until they have gained full strength, then they begin to die by degrees until full death reaches them. They live by instalments and they die by instalments until they die their last death. The child is born with a tongue but does not speak, with hands but does not work, with feet but does not walk, with eyes but sees only very little and does not understand what he sees. The inability to do something is death in relation to it.

"We grow up and perform things we could not do when we were young. But our strength is on the wane. I, myself, I have not been able to climb mount Ṣannīn for years, so I died as a man who could climb the mountain. Most of my hands, feet, eyes and ears died with regard to many things I could perform, distances I could walk, colours, forms and sounds I could discern from far. What has died of me is far more than that which is still alive and yet I reckon myself among the living and so do others. No, no, we die, my son, before we die. We live with death since we are born until we die. Yet we abhor death. Death is true. Praise to him who formed...

---

[65] *Sab'ūn* III, 129-134.

"On the morning of the 16th of July water flowed for the first time through the tubes laid out in the tunnel and poured from its opening. For the first time al-Shakhrūb saw limpid water coming in abundance from its bowels to still the thirst of its dwellers and to fill their other needs without efforts to be spent for its supply. My father was among those who saw the water pour and he thanked his Lord for this benefaction which he had wished, dreamt of and prayed for so long. Unheeded by us my father took a sickle and went to a near-by seed-spot and started to collect the corn. He had not reaped the first armful or his strength failed him. He returned to the house and said to Zakiyah, my brother Naǧīb's wife : 'My days are over, my daughter. I am tired and I have harvested only one armful. I want to sleep. Lay out my bed, my daughter' " [66].

The thoughts of his father on life and death occupy an almost unique place in the autobiography. Only one other person's thoughts about life and death are recorded by Nuʿaymah. They are the thoughts of his Scottish roommate in Seattle, who initiated Nuʿaymah into the teachings of theosophy.

What happened outside Nuʿaymah's immediate surroundings received scant attention if at all. World War II is hardly mentioned, and this fact is explained as follows : "The war from the beginning until after its end monopolized a large part of the produce of my pen. My essays in *al-Bayādir* (The Treshing Floors) and *Ṣawt al-ʿālam* (The Voice of the World), *al-Nūr wa al-dayǧūr* (Light and Darkness), and *Fī mahabb al-rīḥ* (Windward) are the best witnesses to that. No wonder for I had to harmonize my view of man as a heavenly seed growing and developing towards divine perfection with the heinous acts and crimes he committed during this period of growth and development" [67].

How little Nuʿaymah cared for political matters is demonstrated by the fact that he did not write one line about the creation of Israel, not about the ensuing wars. The most important political events in the area other than these are summed up in less than one page, and to the civil war of 1958 in Lebanon only cursory reference is made : "As regards the second event about which a word must be said, it happened to me in al-Shakhrūb at one o'clock P.M. the 28th of August 1958, the year in which a wave of disturbances hit Lebanon shaking its pillars. That day I was in al-Shakhrūb..." [68]. Then follows a somewhat detailed account of the accident that befell Nuʿaymah that day.

66 *Sabʿūn* III, 132-133.
67 *Sabʿūn* III, 173.
68 *Sabʿūn* III, 224-225.

In this third volume also space has been given to Nu'aymah's literary activities. Most of his efforts went into talks produced for special occasions or for radio transmission. Apart from that he wrote the biography of Ğibrān. The controversies that arose after its publication form the subject matter of one of the chapters of this third volume. The open letter written by Amīn al-Rayḥānī has been quoted in full, as was Nu'aymah's public answer [69]. *The Book of Mirdad* is given much attention and the process of its generation described in some detail. The other novels *Liqā'* (Until we meet) and "The Memoirs of Pitted Face" also received their amount of space in the autobiography but not to the extent as *The Book of Mirdad*, which Nu'aymah declares to be his best work [70]. In this third book, also, Nu'aymah has made use of the dialogue form, sometimes as a conversation with himself and sometimes as an apostrophe or as a dialogue between two persons. The reader is currently addressed throughout the volume, explicitly as "I told you this story..." or sometimes less explicitly [71].

A good example of apostrophe are the words spoken to Ğibrān at his tomb in Mār Sarkīs, Lebanon. "O God, O God, How we parted, Ğibrān, in the hospital of Saint Vincent in New York and how we meet here. Has it ever occurred to you or to me that we would part as we did more than a year ago and that we would meet as we do today? How often you spoke to me about Mār Sarkīs. How much you wished for yourself and for me this wonderful recluse. Now you occupy it alone" [72]. One of the instances of a dialogue with himself occurs after he had heard about the fatal illness of his brother Nasīb : "That is a heavy blow, Mīkhā'īl. It is not befitting you to succumb. Everything that is in the Universe is in your thought and heart and in your flesh and blood and it does not harm except those who are ignorant of it, resist it or fight it. Obey it and reconcile yourself with it, willingly and of good heart if you do not want it to crush you. You have come to precipitate conclusions when you thought your material responsibilities towards the family had ended" [73].

Nu'aymah's autobiography is one of the most important works that has come from his pen. Incorporated in it is a biography of the family living in the Lebanese mountain in contrast to Ṭāhā Ḥusayn, *al-Ayyām*, who hardly mentions his parents. Nu'aymah records the vicissitudes of the family in many a passage, and even in the volume about his years in America, he does not forget to relate the fate of his parents, sister and brothers in Lebanon. Unlike Salāmah Mūsā, Nu'aymah has not paid attention

---

69 See footnote 25 of this chapter.
70 *Sab'ūn* III, 209-218 deals with the three books.
71 *Sab'ūn* III, 50, cf. p. 78.
72 *Sab'ūn* III, 77.
73 *Sab'ūn* III, 23.

to world politics or to matters of national importance. Instead he has, among other things, shown part of the rural and intellectual development of Lebanon through the portrait of one family. Unlike Ṭāhā Ḥusayn, Nuʿaymah has not opted for a novelistic treatment, but has tried to achieve some intimacy with the reader by addressing him directly. Together with Ṭāhā Ḥusayn and Salāmah Mūsā, Nuʿaymah introduced new forms of autobiography into Arabic literature.

VI. THE CRITIC

In 1913 Mīkhā'īl Nu'aymah contributed an essay with the title "Fağr al-amal ba'da layl al-ya's" (The Dawn of Hope after the Night of Despair), to the recently established literary magazine *al-Funūn* (The Arts)[1] of his friend Naṣīb 'Arīḍah in New York. "The Dawn of Hope" referred to the first issue of *al-Funūn*, in which next to original Arabic contributions a number of Russian texts in Arabic translation were published. In Nu'aymah's opinion *al-Funūn* marked the beginning of a new era in Arabic literature. His opinion about traditional Arabic literature is voiced in the second half of the title, 'The Night of Despair'. With this essay Nu'aymah made his *début*. It was followed by other essays, which for the greater part were published in *al-Funūn* and subsequently in *al-Sā'iḥ*, which started to function as the mouthpiece of the literary circle round *al-Funūn* when the latter magazine ceased to appear [2].

A choice of Nu'aymah's essays, his prefaces to the *Mağmū'ah* (The Collection) [3] of *Arrabitah* and to his play *al-Ābā' wa al-banūn* (Fathers and Sons) [4], were republished in one volume with the title *al-Ghirbāl* (The Sieve), in Cairo, 1923. 'The Dawn of Hope after the Night of Despair' was not integrally included in this volume, but parts of it were incorporated in another essay forming part of the selection [5]. *Al-Ghirbāl* covers a period of about nine years of Nu'aymah's essayistic activity. It was foreworded by 'Abbās Maḥmūd al-'Aqqād, who, before and simultaneously with Nu'aymah, had expressed some similar thoughts on Arabic literature. In his turn Nu'aymah included reviews of *al-Dīwān* [6] by al-'Aqqād and al-Māzinī and of al-'Aqqād's *al-Fuṣūl* [7] in *al-Ghirbāl*.

1 *al-Funūn* I, 4 (July, 1913), p. 50-70.

2 Cf. Chapter II, footnotes 45, 49 and 61.

3 First published in New York, 1921, reprinted, Beirut, 1964.

4 The play was serialized in *al-Funūn* from December, 1916 onward in the issues II, 8, and following until volume II, number 12 (May, 1917).

5 *Sab'ūn* II, p. 30 footnote 1 where Nu'aymah writes that parts of "The Dawn of Hope etc." were included in "al-Ḥabāḥib" (Fireflies), *al-Ghirbāl*, p. 37-64.

6 'Abbās Maḥmūd al-'Aqqād and Ibrāhīm 'Abd al-Qādir al-Māzinī, *al-Dīwān*, parts I and II, Cairo, 1921. In their foreword the two authors declare that they have a 10-volume work in mind, explaining modern trends in poetry, criticism and writing. The first two volumes, the only ones to appear, however, were devoted to criticism of the work of authors belonging to a former generation. Al-'Aqqād concentrated his attack on Aḥmad Shawqī, called the Prince of Poetry, and al-Māzinī spent his anger on his former friend, 'Abd al-Raḥmān Shukrī and subjected Muṣṭafā Luṭfī al-Manfalūṭī to some severe criticism. See also : A. M. K. Al-Zubaidi, 'The Dīwān School', *Journal of Arabic Literature*, Vol. I, 1970, p. 36 ff.

7 *Al-Fuṣūl* was first published in Cairo, 1922.

With some reservations the contents of the essays of *al-Ghirbāl* can be brought under two headings : 'Literary Theory' and 'Literary Criticism' [8]. The latter category corresponds more or less with the second half of the book. It comprises reviews of various books and publications, such as an unpublished *dīwān* by Nu'aymah's friend, Nasīb 'Arīḍah [9]; a poem by Aḥmad Shawqī [10]; a volume of poetry by the Lebanese emigrant Rashīd Salīm al-Khūrī [11]; a volume of English poetry by Amīn al-Rayḥānī [12]; the English prose-poem 'The Forerunner' by Ğibrān [13]; the Arabic translation by Miss Mārī Ziyādah of Max Müller's *Deutsche Liebe* [14] as well as a lecture delivered by her; a volume of early poetry by Muḥammad al-Shurayqī [15]; a book on geniality by Labīb al-Riyāshī [16]; a translation of the *Merchant of Venice* by Khalīl Muṭrān [17]; Ğibran's *al-'Awāṣif* (The Tempests) [18]; and the two volumes mentioned, *al-Dīwān* and *al-Fuṣūl.*

Strictly speaking, not all the essays of the first half of the book come under the heading of Literary Theory. Moreover, the reviews in the second half of *al-Ghirbāl* are not without thoughts on the theory of literature. Yet the term seems adequate, since the essays coming under it are theoretical, deal with literature in general, and do not have a specific work of art as their subject.

In later volumes Nu'aymah only occasionally returned to literary subjects. One essay in each of the volumes *al-Marāḥil* [19] (Stages), *Zād al-ma'ād* [20] (Food for the Road),

---

8 The distinction drawn here is the one made by Wellek and Warren, *Theory of Literature.* Harmondsworth, 1963³, p. 39.

9 "*al-Arwāḥ al-ḥā'irah*" (Souls Benumbed) was eventually published in 1946 in New York, shortly after Nasīb 'Arīḍah had died in April 1946. He lived, however, long enough to see it printed. *Sab'ūn* III, p. 177.

10 The poem criticised was the one Shawqī delivered on the occasion of the establishment of a "Society for the Co-ordination of Help for the Poor". The poem was published afterwards in *al-Hilāl,* April, 1920.

11 Rashīd Salīm al-Khūrī, better known under his pen-name *al-Shā'ir al-qarawī* (The Village Poet), published his *al-Qarawiyyāt* (Village Poems) in Sao Paolo, 1922. Information taken from *al-Ghirbāl,* p. 155.

12 Amīn al-Rayḥānī, *A Chant of Mystics and Other Poems.* New York, 1921. Information derived from *al-Ghirbāl,* 163, footnote.

13 *The Forerunner* was first published in New York, 1920.

14 Mārī Ziyādah, better known as al-Ānisah Mayy (Miss Mayy) published her translation of *Deutsche Liebe* with the title *Ibtisāmāt wa dumū'* (Smiles and Tears). The second impression. Cairo, 1922, is reviewed by Nu'aymah. Information derived from *al-Ghirbāl,* p. 178.

15 *Aghānī al-Ṣibā* (Songs of Childhood), Damascus, 1921.

16 *al-Nubūgh* (The Genius), Beirut, 1921.

17 Muṭrān's translation *Tāğir al-bunduqiyyah* was published in Cairo, 1922.

18 *al-'Awāṣif,* Cairo, 1920.

19 "al-Wāḥah al-ḥayyah" (The Living Oasis), *al-Marāḥil,* Beirut, 1966⁴, p. 104-111. 1st impr. 1933.

20 "Dā' al-adab" (The Disease of Literature), *Zād al-ma'ād,* Beirut, 1962³, p. 51-54, 1st impr. Cairo, 1936.

and *al-Awthān* [21] (The Idols), two in *al-Durūb* [22] (Roads) and three in *Fī mahabb al-rīḥ* [23] (Windward) may be counted on this score. Otherwise Nu'aymah seems to have abandoned literary theory in favour of a theory of life.

Nu'aymah's appreciation of traditional Arabic literature was conditioned to some extent by the literary climate of his host countries. There he became acquainted with the great works of European literature and with literary theory as it had developed after Wordsworth and Shelley. Impressed by his readings of European letters, Nu'aymah described all Arab authors, the greatest among them not excluded, as fireflies, compared to the giants of European literature : "... I do not think that you will be so hardy as to raise one of them to equality with Homer, Virgil, Dante, Shakespeare, Milton, Byron, Hugo, Zola, Goethe, Heine and Tolstoy. They [the Arab poets] lived and died to sing of the doe of the desert, the scintillating swords, the cantering horses, the spilling of blood, the course of the camel, the remains of the camp, the fire of the guestmeals etc." [24]. Nu'aymah obviously became dissatisfied with Arabic poetry and with everything that bound it to its traditional course. Not only the old panegyric and its pendants, the satire (*hiǧā'*) and the elegy (*marthiyyah*) in *qaṣīdah* form or not, came under his fire, but also the presses which opened their columns to these products. He scorned the press for its ample use of *epitheta ornantia* to introduce known or unknown poets to the readers. "... everybody who thinks himself a poet hardly has composed his first poem or you see that papers and magazines have opened their hearts to him and have furnished him with *epitheta* varying between 'genius' and 'excellent modern poet'. Even our poorest poet is, if not a genius, at least an excellent modern poet" [25].

The brunt of Nu'aymah's attack was directed against the high estimate the formal constituents of poetry, such as metre and rhyme, enjoyed, and against the much admired use of archaic words. At the same time he broke a lance for the invention of neologisms and for an occasional deviation from the grammatical rules. "Their poet

---

[21] "*al-Kalimah as-sawdā'*" (The Black Word = "In Black and White" or "In Writing"), *al-Awthān*, Beirut, 1962⁴, p. 44-48, 1st impr. 1946.

[22] "Māhiyyat al-adab wa muhimmatuhu" (The Essence and Importance of Literature), *al-Durūb*, Beirut, 1966⁴, p. 36-59; "al-Adīb wa al-nāqid" (The Literary Man and the Critic), *al-Durūb*, p. 170-189.

[23] "al-Adīb wa al-dawlah" (Literature and the State), *Fī mahabb al-rīḥ*, Beirut, 1962³, p. 96-104; "Awzār al-lughah" (The Burdens of the Language), p. 125-132; "Maǧd al-qalam" (The Glory of the Pen), p. 172-177.

[24] "al-Ḥabāḥib" (The Fireflies), *al-Ghirbāl*, p, 48.

[25] "al-Shi'r wa al-shā'ir" (Poetry and the Poet), *al-Ghirbāl*, p. 88. Nu'aymah wrote words of similar purport in "al-Maqāyīs al-adabiyyah" (The Literary Yardsticks), *al-Ghirbāl*, p. 73.

is one, who, when poetizing, does not lapse in the metre, nor transgresses the monorhyme and who does not choose but words difficult to understand except for those who spent their lifes studying the Arabic language only". [26]

In the essay "al-Ziḥāfāt wa al-ʿilal" [27] (Substitutions and Inversions), subtitled "al-Shiʿr wa al-ʿarūḍ" (Poetry and Prosody) Nuʿaymah once more dealt with the rules of Arabic prosody. Making use of the fact that one and the same Arabic word *baḥr* denotes 'metre' as well as 'sea' he developed the ready metaphore to its absurd end as an expression of his contempt for the intricacies in Arabic verse. "One of the graces of the prosody, my friend, is that it has many seas (= metres). Every one of these seas has its boats without which it is not possible for you to sail on it. All these boats have oars which cannot be used except in them and all the oars have their tholes, their bends and grips which are unknown except to him who has a rich experience and a long patience. Therefore, to sail on these seas one must plunge into dangers and stake one's life" [28]. The complexity of Arabic prosody is reflected in statements in which the time and energy spent on them in the classroom is deplored [29].

Al-ʿAqqad, following the English romantics, wrote words of a similar purport in 1911, in his *Khulāṣat al-yawmiyyah* (The Quitessence of the Diary). "The poet is not some body who just balances periods — that is a poetaster or somebody who does not write prose... The poet is he who feels and makes (us) feel" [30].

Already in 1905 Ǧurǧī Zaydān wrote words to this effect in *al-Hilāl*, commenting upon the prose poems of al-Rayḥānī : "Poetry according to the Arabs is rhymed, metrical speech. If it is otherwise they do not consider it to be poetry, as if they define with regards to words and not to meaning" [31]. What Nuʿaymah wrote, therefore, was not completely unheard of in literary criticism. Moreover, he had gained first-hand knowledge of Arabic poetry in prose through his relationship with Ǧibrān and al-Rayḥānī. And it is not unlikely that he was acquainted with the poetry and theories of Walt Whitman [32].

---

26 "Naqīq al-ḍafādiʿ" (The Croaking of the Frogs), *al-Ghirbāl*, p. 99.

27 *al-Ghirbāl*, p. 107-125 "*Ziḥāfah*" (pl. *Ziḥāfāt*) denotes the change of the verse foot by the retraction of one letter, but may be used as well to denote other changes of the verse foot. "*ʿillah*" (pl. *ʿilal*) is used for any change in the verse foot.

28 "al-Ziḥāfāt wa al-ʿilal", *al-Ghirbāl*, p. 109.

29 "al-Ziḥāfāt wa al-ʿilal", *al-Ghirbāl*, p. 119.

30 "*Innamā al-shāʿir man yashʿur wa yushʿir*", *Khulāṣat al-yawmiyyah* (Excerpt of the Diary), Beirut, 1970, p. 120. The first edition of this work was published in Cairo, 1911. A reprint appeared in Cairo, 1968.

31 *al -Hilāl*, XIV, 2 (November, 1905), p. 97.

32 Cf. S. Moreh, 'Poetry in Prose (*al-Shiʿr al-Manthūr*) in Modern Arabic Literature', *Middle*

Nu'aymah's opinions about the necessity of metre and rhyme show some variety. In "al-Ziḥāfat wa al-'ilal" (Substitutions and Inversions) he compares metres and rhymes with rites and abodes of worship, which are, according to him superfluous with regard to devotion [33]. In "al-Shi'r wa al-shā'ir" (Poetry and the Poet) he not only mentions that metre and rhyme belong to the constituent elements of poetry, but that metre is essential. Comparing the poet to the musician he writes : "... he [the poet] hears harmonic sounds where we hear rumbling and grumbling only ... Therefore he gives expression to them in measured, singing phrases" [34].

The essay "Naqīq al-ḍafādi'" [35] (The Croaking of the Frogs) is a defense of innovations in vocabulary. It seems directed in the first place against those who criticized the *Mahǧarī* (Emigrant) poets for the impurities that had crept into their language. Nu'aymah solves the problem by declaring language a kind of thesaurus of imperfect symbols : "... it belongs to ill-luck of mankind that you see them forced to make use of symbols to express the workings of life in them, because the symbol is in its best and subtlest frame no more than a faint shade of what it refers to" [36]. Nu'aymah concludes that language does not have an independent value. In Nu'aymah's view the poet's creation of new words and structures is not only legitimate, but also a prerequisite for the survival of the language [37]. Emerson's poet "as the namer or language maker" [38] seems to have been rendered into Arabic.

Al-'Aqqād held different views. While describing words as symbols he stressed the evocative character of them being capable not only of translating thoughts and feelings, but also of calling them forth : "Words are a kind of abridged meanings which point to what cannot be brought on the tongue; or they are symbols each of which is connected with thoughts and associations that occur to the mind when that word touches it. No other word participates therein, not even apparent synonyms" [39]. The word is not a hazy reference to meaning for al-'Aqqād. Its evocative power with regard to its meaning differs in strength only in accordance with its connotations with the hearer. To al-'Aqqād language is a far more precise instrument than to

---

Eastern Studies, Vol. 4, 4 (July, 1968), p. 330-360. Nu'aymah mentions the poetry of Walt Whitman in "al-Shi'r wa al-shā'ir", *al-Ghirbāl*, p. 85.

33 "al-Ziḥāfāt wa al-'ilal" (Substitutions and Inversions) *al-Ghirbāl*, esp. p. 116.

34 "al-Shi'r wa al-shā'ir", *al-Ghirbāl*, p. 84 f.

35 *al-Ghirbāl*, p. 90-106.

36 "Naqīq al-ḍafādi'", *al-Ghirbāl*, p. 103.

37 "Naqīq al-ḍafādi'", *al-Ghirbāl*, p. 98 and p. 106.

38 Ralph Waldo Emerson, 'The Poet', *Essays* 1st and 2nd series, London, Everyman's Library, ed. 1907, p. 215.

39 *Khulāṣat al-yawmiyyah*, Beirut, 1970, p. 16; Cairo ed., 1968, p. 20.

Nuʿaymah, and therefore al-ʿAqqād demands the utmost care in keeping the Arabic language pure and uncorrupted [40].

Faced with Nuʿaymah's theories in *al-Ghirbāl*, al-ʿAqqād took up the challenge and explained his point of view in the preface. "We must remember," he wrote, "that the language has not been created today so that we may create its bases and roots as we go along. Development occurs only in languages which have no past, nor bases and roots" [41].

Next to his efforts to make clear what is non-essential in poetry, Nuʿaymah tried to formulate an answer to the question "What is poetry?". His postulate seems to have been "poetry is boundless" [42]. This may mean that poetry is pluriform, but also that it is beyond human reasoning. The latter notion dominates Nuʿaymah's theories. Independent from it stands the fact that his thoughts on the subject did not lead him to anything like a systematized theory. The reason for this must be sought in Nuʿaymah's interest to convert poets to another, more romantic, concept of poetry. Such a goal requires a propagandist more than a theoretician.

Nuʿaymah's central idea is that literature originates in the human soul. The idea may not seem very original now, but in the Arabic literary circles of the time it was a topic of some importance. Muṣṭafā Luṭfī al-Manfalūṭī wrote in this vein in his *Naẓarāt* when he said that the poet reveals his soul as it is to the listener [43], and that the literary utterance means the giving of a true picture of a meaning present in the soul [44]. Al-ʿAqqād described poetry as the interpreter of the soul [45]. He may even have thought of poetry as an unrestrained effusion of the soul, when he portrayed the poet as quickly touched and swayed by the feelings of the moment [46]. In Nuʿaymah's thought a sort of incubation period precedes the actual poetic creation, which in its turn overcomes the poet as childbirth overcomes a pregnant woman [47].

---

40 The late Muḥammad Mandūr, *al-Naqd wa al-nuqqād al-muʿāṣirīn* (Criticism and Contemporary Critics), Cairo (between 1957 and 1959), p. 47, holds that, contrary to Nuʿaymah's thesis, the literary language is more adequate in the rendering of human emotions than the colloquial, which, he asserts, is used only in connection with the prime necessities of life.

41 "Muqaddimat al-Ṭabʿ al-Ūlā"' (Foreword to the First Edition), *al-Ghirbāl*, p. 11.

42 "al-Shiʿr wa al-shāʿir" (Poetry and the Poet), *al-Ghirbāl*, p. 76, and "al-Ziḥāfāt wa al-ʿilal", *al-Ghirbāl*, p. 112.

43 "al-Shiʿr" (Poetry), *al-Naẓarāt* (Views) II, 1925[5] (Cairo), p. 300. The first impression of *al-Naẓarāt* (3 vols.) must date from between 1902 and 1910.

44 "al-Bayān" (Rhetorics), *al-Naẓarāt* III, Cairo, 1923[4], p. 7.

45 Foreword by al-ʿAqqād for the second part of Shukrī's *dīwān*, 1913. Al-ʿAqqād's words occur on p. 97 of the complete *dīwān* edition published in 1960 in Alexandria.

46 *Khulāṣat al-yawmiyyah*, 1st ed., 1911, p. 52 of the Beirut edition of 1970.

47 "al-Ziḥāfāt wa al-ʿilal", *al-Ghirbāl*, p. 124.

Like Wordsworth, Nu'aymah considers thoughts and feelings the raw materials of poetry. Nu'aymah, however, does not follow Wordsworth in the latter's concept of thoughts modifying and directing the feelings. In Nu'aymah's writings thoughts and feelings seem to be self-willed and autonomous, mixing with but not affecting each other. The poet may exert his critical power over rhymes and phrases, but thoughts and feelings figure as a kind of archetypes in his construction. In "al-Shi'r wa al-shā'ir" (Poetry and the Poet) he writes : "The poet — we mean the poet not the versifier — does not grasp the pen unless driven by an inner agent beyond his control. He is a slave in this respect. But he is an absolute ruler when he sets himself to cut out for his feelings and thoughts statues of phrases and rhymes, because he selects them to his wont" [48].

The thoughts and feelings are God's creation and their independence of human zeal is stressed by Nu'aymah's introduction of the realms of absolute thought and free feeling into his argument [49]. A concept like this leaves little hope for an adequate rendering by man. The symbols used by man, Nu'aymah writes, give but a faint and enigmatic reflection of them [Thoughts and feelings] [50]. Yet, Nu'aymah holds that poems can give full expression to thoughts and feelings through what may be called "the unsaid". What the symbols, i.e. vocabulary, grammar and prosody, cannot render, can be read between the lines [51]. Nu'aymah seems not to have perceived that the unsaid can function only through what has been said and, therefore, can never be independent of the symbols man has at his disposal.

Another pair of words, originating from Plato and used by Shelley and Emerson, are "the true and the beautiful". After mentioning as the first need of man that of expression (*ifṣāḥ*) of what influences his soul, Nu'aymah introduces secondly the concept of the true and the beautiful in his essay on literary yardsticks.

"First : Our need to give expression to all the stirrings of the soul that befall us : hope and despair, victory and defeat, belief and doubt, love and aversion, pleasure and pain, sadness and mirth, fear and ease of mind and all the emotions and sensations fluctuating between the most extreme and the nearest of these stirrings.

"Second : Our need for light to guide us in life. There is no light to guide us except the light of truth, the truth in ourselves and the truth in the world around us. Though we differ in our understanding of it, we cannot deny that in life is something which was true in the time of Adam, which is still so today, and which will remain true into the end of times.

---

48 "al-Shi'r wa al-shā'ir", *al-Ghirbāl*, p. 86.

49 "Naqīq al-ḍafādi'", *al-Ghirbāl*, p. 102.

50 "Naqīq al-ḍafādi'", *al-Ghirbāl*, p. 103.

51 "Naqīq al-ḍafādi'", *al-Ghirbāl*, p. 102.

"Third : Our need for the beautiful in everything. There is an unquenchable thirst in the spirit for the beautiful, and everything having an aspect of beauty. Though our tastes may differ in what we consider beautiful or ugly, we cannot pretend to be blind to the fact that there exists absolute beauty in life, on which no two tastes will differ.

"Fourth : Our need for music. In the spirit is a strange, incomprehensible penchant for voices and melodies. It [the spirit] is quickened by the rolling of the thunder, the murmuring of water, the rustling of leaves, but it winces at inharmonious sounds and is set at ease and comforted by what it is accustomed to" [52].

"The True and the Beautiful" occur also in the essay "al-Shi'r wa al-shā'ir" [53] (The Poetry and the Poet) in *al-Ghirbāl* and it returns in the later volumes *Zād al-ma'ād* [54] (Food for the Road) and *Durūb* [55] (Roads). Nu'aymah's dealings with the pair in this last volume are interesting. Here he introduces the notions of absolute beauty, absolute truth and absolute good to emphasize the imperfection of human appreciation. "Beauty, the true and the good — these three words recur from the pens and the tongues of authors and critics whenever they speak about the value and the message of literature. The critic reviewing a literary work has to know the true; he should be able to distinguish the good; and he should have a thorough knowledge of all the characteristics of beauty, in order to be qualified to pronounce a verdict over that work. But such a critic does not exist al all. Nobody knows the whole truth; nor can he isolate the integral good; nor can he embrace complete beauty. As regards our perceptions we are still in the realms of relativity" [56].

Not only the true, the good and the beautiful are treated by Nu'aymah as independent entities, similar to thoughts and feelings, but he also believes that poetry has an existence separate from the poems in which it appears, as may be seen in his rather lyrical description in the essay "al-Shi'r wa al-shā'ir" : "Poetry is the victory of light over darkness, of truth over untruth; it is the singing of the nightingale; the plaint of the dove; the rustle of the brook; and the rolling of the thunder; it is the smile of the child and the tear of the woman who lost her child; the flowering of the virgin's cheek and the wrinkles in the face of the old man; it is the beauty of survival and the survival of beauty. Poetry is the tasting of the joy of life and the shivering before the face of death; it is love and hatred; opulence and misery; it is the cry of the wretch-

52 "al-Maqāyīs al-adabiyyah" (The Literary Yardsticks), *al-Ghirbāl*, p. 70 f.

53 *al-Ghirbāl*, p. 80. The "True" and the "Beautiful" figure here in a somewhat expanded group, which comprises "Justice" and "The Good" (*al-ğamāl, al-'adl, al-ḥaqq, al-khayr*).

54 "Dā' al-adab" (The Disease of Literature), *Zād al-ma'ād* (Food for the Road), p. 51-54.

55 "al-Adīb wa al-nāqid" (The Literary Man and the Critic), *Durūb* (Roads), p. 170-189.

56 "al-Adīb wa al-nāqid", *Durūb*, p. 177 f.

ed, the laughter of the drunkard, the complaint of the weak, the vanity of the strong — Poetry is an overpowering craving, a constant longing for a world we do not and will not know; it is an everlasting attraction to embrace the whole universe, and to unite with all minerals, plants and animals in it; it is the spiritual essence extending until its outer ends touch the extremes of the essence of the world. In short, poetry is life weeping and laughing, lamenting and jubilating, complaining and praising, accepting and turning away" [57].

The distinction between ideal and phenomenal poetry is explicitly drawn in Nu'aymah's review of Nasīb al-'Arīḍah's *al-Arwāḥ al-ḥā'irah.* Nu'aymah begins this review as follows : "Poetry — with regards to its origin — is one. It is immeasurable, indivisible, unvariable, because the origin of poetry is life, and life is the same in the gnat, in the camel and in the lion. But as regards its manifestation poetry is, as life, diversified, multicoloured and graduated" [58]. According to Nu'aymah, the reader may consider one poem more beautiful than another on the basis of its form, "but the poetry of the first and of the second is one, without preference or difference in value" [59]. The quality of phenomenal poetry thus comes to depend on the quantity of ideal poetry used in its making as may be concluded from the following lines : "While we see it [Poetry] in some of its manifestations as a small pond, we see it in others as a brook gliding between the sands, or again as a tumultuous river in which brooks pour out, or as a boiling sea in which the rivers stream, or finally as a wide ocean in which the seas meet. We prefer the ocean to the pond not because the water of the ocean is more beautiful and nobler than that of the pond, but because the ocean has an extension which the pond has not" [60].

On the whole, however, Nu'aymah stresses the function of poetry as a receptacle and vehicle of meaning, as Shukrī and al-'Aqqād had done before him in Egypt. Shukrī's approach is the more emotional, as is revealed in his preface to the third part of his *dīwān* : "The great poet is not content by making people understand; he tries to dope them and to possess them..." [61]. Nu'aymah is more speculative in his theory than al-'Aqqād, who wrote in his *Khulāṣat al-yawmiyyah* : "Poetry is the craft of producing feelings by means of speech" [62]. And in the foreword to the

57 "al-Shi'r wa al-shā'ir", *al-Ghirbāl,* p. 76 f.

58 "al-Arwāḥ al-ḥā'irah, *al-Ghirbāl,* p. 127.

59 "al-Arwāḥ al-ḥā'irah", *al-Ghirbāl,* p. 128.

60 "al-Arwāḥ al-ḥā'irah", *al-Ghirbāl,* p. 128.

61 Foreword to the third part of his *dīwān.* Alexandria, 1960, p. 209.

62 *Khulāṣat al-yawmiyyah,* p. 15.

second part of Shukrī's dīwān he described poetry as a "reliable transmitter of her [the soul's] tongue" [63].

Nu'aymah also considers literature to be a messenger between the soul of the poet and somebody else's soul [64]. He elaborates this idea in the essay 'Naqīq al-ḍafādi', harmonizing it with the idea of archetypal thought and feeling. He describes the poet as "Stretching out the hidden fingers of his inspiration to the coverings of your hearts and thoughts to lift up an edge of them, and to turn your glances to what lies folded up underneath so that you will see feelings and stumble over thoughts. At first you will reckon them to be thoughts and feelings of the poet. They are in reality your feelings and thoughts which the poet did not invent, create or wake up. He only lifted up a tip of the veil and directed all your glances towards them" [65]. Arnold's concept of adding to one's store of thoughts and feelings seems at a far remove, since Nu'aymah's poet reveals only what is already there [66].

In another context, however, Nu'aymah leaves more room for a concept like Arnold's when he declares that "Humanity travels with poetry as its companion, its consolator, its spender of encouragement and its fortifyer" [67]. He is sharing the thoughts of more than one Western critic when he says that the poet "should prepare a useful lesson out of every aspect of life" [68]. Nu'aymah seems to be bordering on Arnold's ideas when he interprets this useful lesson in a gnostic sense, whereas Arnold preferred an intimate interrelation between religion and poetry. Not only in poetry, but in everything man does, Nu'aymah writes, "... he is after one thing. That is to reveal himself to himself in order to understand the forces by which he is set in motion on the sea of being. A work he undertakes has value only in sofar as it brings man nearer to or farther away from the knowledge of the self" [69]. Seen within the context of Nu'aymah's equation of the soul, or the self, with God, as well as within his theory of the ultimate union of man and God through the perfection of knowledge, one is tempted to interpret the knowledge of the self in terms of gnosis. To Nu'aymah poetry could be a complete *magister vitae* as it is to Arnold [70].

---

[63] Shukrī, *Dīwān*, p. 97.

[64] "Miḥwar al-adab" (The Pivot of Literature), *al-Ghirbāl*, p. 27 : "Therefore, literature which is literature is nothing but a messenger between the soul of the author and the soul of another person.

[65] "Naqīq al-ḍafādi'", *al-Ghirbāl*, p. 102.

[66] M. Arnold, *Selected Prose* edited by P. J. Keating, Harmondsworth, 1970, p. 413 in his letter of about March 1, 1849 to his friend Hugh Clough. Arnold writes : "On the other hand, there are two offices of poetry — one to add to one's store of thoughts and feelings — another to compose and elevate the mind by a sustained tone, numerous allusions, and a grand style".

[67] "al-Shi'r wa al-shā'ir", *al-Ghirbāl*, p. 77.

[68] "al-Ḥabāḥib" (The Fireflies), *al-Ghirbāl*, p. 50.

[69] "Miḥwar al-adab" (The Pivot of Literature), *al-Ghirbāl*, p. 25.

[70] Cf. M. Arnold's letter of October 28, 1852 to A. H. Clough, in M. Arnold, *Selected Prose*, p. 417.

Last, but not least, Nu'aymah has something to say about criticism itself. He is dissatisfied with the way in which it is frequently practised in Arabic literature. He did not stand alone in this. In 1918 a certain Ḥasan al-Sharīf had voiced a similar protest in *al-Hilāl*: "Our ignorance of the art of criticism has brought us so far that we do not know the difference between criticism on the one hand and eulogy or obloquy on the other" [71]. Nu'aymah's view is to be found in "al-Gharbalah" (The Sifting), the opening essay of *al-Ghirbāl* [72]. Some hints of it are to be seen in his review of *al-Dīwān*, in which he rebukes al-'Aqqād and al-Māzinī for their rough treatment of poets, instead of confining themselves to criticizing their words [73]. Nu'aymah shows some sympathy, however, for the scathing remarks of al-'Aqqād against Shawqī, because the latter should have wasted his talent on a commercial poem [74].

In "al-Gharbalah" (The Sifting), Nu'aymah demands that the literary critic separate the work of art from its author for the sake of criticism. The underlying thought may be summarized as bad poetry does not make a man stupid nor does a scoundrel necessarily write inferior poetry [75]. Neither historical criticism, nor the rising opposition against it, seems to have exerted any influence on Nu'aymah's opinion, as this trend of criticism lay well outside his province.

Another major idea of Nu'aymah is that the critic, by guiding the poet may be able to bring him to a better use of his talents [76]. Nu'aymah's approach to criticism is rather ethical, it seems, as may be inferred also from the direction into which he wants the poet to be guided. The poet is to be deflected from the rules of prosody and language as determinants of poetry, and instead to be led back to his self. He should learn to discover poetic self-sufficiency of thoughts and feelings [77].

As regards the scale of values to be used by the critic, Nu'aymah refrains from being prescriptive. While he recognizes the existence of absolute beauty and truth, of ideal poetry, and of absolute thoughts and feelings, he does not admit of absolute rules. The availability of such basic rules would make the critic superfluous, as everybody would be able to see for himself what has value and what not [78]. Nu'aymah's critic is thrown back upon his own resources as he is required to develop a set

---

71 "Nahḍat al-adab fī Miṣr" (The Renaissance of Literature in Egypt), *al-Hilāl*, Vol. 27 (1918), p. 67 ff.

72 "al-Gharbalah", *al-Ghirbāl*, p. 13-15.

73 "al-Dīwān", *al-Ghirbāl*, p. 217.

74 "al-Dīwān", *al-Ghirbāl*, p. 214.

75 "al-Gharbalah", *al-Ghirbāl*, p. 13-15.

76 "al-Gharbalah", *al-Ghirbāl*, p. 19.

77 "al-Ziḥāfāt wa al-'ilal", *al-Ghirbāl*, p. 125.

78 "al-Gharbalah", *al-Ghirbāl*, p. 17.

of yardsticks for himself, and not to use those made by others [79]. The quality of such rods naturally depends on the ability of the critic, specified by Nuʻaymah as "how much pure intention, love of the craft, zeal for the subject, fine taste, subtle perception and alertness of thought, he puts into his lines, and after that what rhetorical talents he has received to convey his sayings to the mind and heart of the reader" [80].

Unsystematized as they may be, Nuʻaymah's views have probably exerted some influence on nascent Arab literary theory. It is probable that *al-Ghirbāl* served as a signpost pointing to Western critical methods, of which Nuʻaymah was one of the first to catch a glimpse.

[79] "al-Gharbalah", *al-Ghirbāl*, p. 17.
[80] "al-Gharbalah", *al-Ghirbāl*, p. 16.

VII. THE PREACHER

Nuʿaymah relates in his autobiography *Sabʿūn*, that he shared his room with a Scottish student during the third year of his studies at the University in Seattle [1]. This student happened to be a member of the Theosophical Society. Through him Nuʿaymah became acquainted with a set of beliefs which left their mark on almost everything he wrote afterwards. He adopted, it seems, at least the first two of the three basic points of theosophy as they are mentioned by Madame Blavatsky in *The Key to Theosophy* :

1. Belief in one absolute incomprehensible and supreme Deity, or infinite essence, which is the root of all nature, and all that is, visible and invisible.
2. Belief in man's eternal immortal nature, which, being a radiation of the Universal Soul, is of an identical essence with it [2].

Mme Blavatsky's third point was not followed by Nuʿaymah at least not in his writings. A faint parallel to Mme Blavatsky's assertion that "real divine theurgy requires superhuman purity and holiness of life", may perhaps be found in Nuʿaymah's belief in the ultimate omnipotence of man as a result of the purification of his thoughts and his heart, and of his faith in man as the image of God and in his [man's] distant and exalted goal [3].

Notwithstanding his theosophical inclinations, Nuʿaymah nowhere in his writings refers to one of the important theoreticians of the Theosophical Society, nor to any of their works. But he does mention works which enjoyed a growing interest in the years before and after the beginning of the twentieth century.

In his autobiography Nuʿaymah writes how he became acquainted with the *Bhagavad Gita* and with Swami Vivekananda's *Raja Yoga* some time after 1925, when he was employed by the organizer of an oriental exhibition in New York [4]. During a business visit to Philadelphia he chanced upon Lau Tsu's *Tau-te-king* (or *Tau-te-tsing*) [5]. He freely quotes from this work in his essay "The Face of Lao Tsu" [6]. The translation

---

[1] *Sabʿūn* II, p. 44 ff.

[2] H. P. Blavatsky, *The Key to Theosophy*. 3rd and revised English edition. London, 1893, p. 2.

[3] "Risālat al-sharq al-mutağaddid" (The Message of the Renovated East), *Durūb*, p. 64.

[4] *Sabʿūn* II, p. 241 f.

[5] "al-Muwağğih al-aʿẓam" (The Supreme Director), *al-Nūr wa al-dayğūr*, p. 143 f. J. J. L. Duyvendak, *Tau-te-tsing. Het boek van de weg en deugd uit het Chinees vertaald en toegelicht*. Arnhem, 1942.

[6] Nuʿaymah, "Wağh Lao Tsū" (The Face of Lao Tze), *al-Marāḥil*, p. 16-29.

Nu'aymah had at hand, however, shows some fundamental differences with the one made by the late J. J. L. Duyvendak, as far as can be judged from Nu'aymah's quotations. In comparison to Duyvendak's wise man, Nu'aymah's sage is closer to the people, and he is not advised to keep them ignorant [7].

His education in a Russian seminary was not lost to Nu'aymah, as can be observed in his many references and allusions to the Bible. His explanations of Biblical stories, however, are not always free from theosophical influence. The Sermon of the Mount is his favourite part of the Bible, as he more than once states in his autobiography. Largely in line with this sermon are Tolstoy's ethical teachings, which Nu'aymah admired, as he likewise declares in his autobiography. This admiration for Tolstoy seems to culminate in the latter's professed adversity to, and final foresaking of, the goods of this world. It is at least the one thing of substance Nu'aymah says about Tolstoy's ethics [8].

Nu'aymah did not really develop a philosophical system of his own as his observation that *The Book of Mirdad* is the summit of his thought might lead one to think [9]. He did not systematize his thoughts in a separate work, for one thing. Also a consistent philosophy cannot be distilled from his works. Most of the essays were written down for large audiences, and Nu'aymah reveals himself in these writings as a popular thinker and preacher who does not care too much for details or for systems, as long as he can make his point. This does not mean that Nu'aymah's thought is unsystematic, but that it is impossible to set up a system in which all his ideas fit.

In Nu'aymah's 'system' God is the beginning and end of everything. This God is the creator of all things, seen and unseen, and at the same time He established the order governing His creation : "There is one order", he writes, "that is the order by which the creator bound his creation" [10]. In a later publication Nu'aymah uses the "Universal Order" (*al-Niẓām al-kawnī*) as an alternative to the term "God". He says he

---

7 Duyvendak translates : "The more useful tools people possess, the more upheaval in states" (p. 90). The alternative translation given by Duyvendak in his notes (p. 175) as "scherpe wapenen" seems to have been used in the translation which is at the base of Nu'aymah's version. He uses the word *asliḥah* (*al-Marāḥil*, p. 24), which means "arms", though it may denote "tools" in certain contexts. Where Duyvendak's translation warns against "too many clever craftsmen" (p. 90), Nu'aymah lays the blame on "artfulness and cunning" (*dahā' wa iḥtiyāl*), p. 24). Duyvendak translates : "He treats them (i.e. the prince treats the people) as infants" (p. 78 : "de heilige behandelt hen allen als onmondige kinderen"), which is rendered by Nu'aymah as "He treats them as if they were his sons" (p. 25).

8 *Sab'ūn* I, p. 269 ff.

9 *Sab'ūn* III, p. 213.

10 "Bu'bu' al-adab" (The bugbear of literature), *al-Marāḥil*, p. 117.

prefers the first term as an answer to the question "Who is He — or what is it — that rules mankind and the rulers of mankind and everything that is in the endless cosmos?" [11] He shows panentheistic inclinations when he calls the universe "the living body of God" [12], or when he describes nature as "the visible body of God" [13].

Man is an indivisible part of the universe, as Nu'aymah writes in the essay "The Enchantment of Being" : "... you do not know or pretend not to know that you and the cosmos (*al-kawn*) are an indivisible unity. The cosmos has been food for you, only in order that you will be food for it. Its spirit has been your spirit, only that your spirit will be its spirit. Its body was your body, only that your body will be its body. If you would be one with it as it is with you, you would be in a perpetual state of intoxication by the enchantment of being" [14].

On the other hand man is a drop of divine semen, according to Nu'aymah in another essay : 'This drop comprises all divine faculties from omniscience to omnipotence... like any seed comprises all the qualities of the plant it brings forth" [15]. Or, as Nu'aymah writes in *The Book of Mirdad* : "Man is a God in swaddling-bands. Time is a swaddling-band. Space is a swaddling-band. Flesh is a swaddling-band, and likewise all the senses and the things perceivable therewith. The mother knows too well that the swaddling-bands are not the babe. The babe, however, knows it not" [16].

The essential godliness of man is a prerequisite for the knowledge of God, Nu'aymah argues : "If the prophets had not been certain of God's being in every man, it would have been less stupid of them to lecture on art before stones and on philosophy before monkeys than to preach God to creatures empty of God" [17]. He epitomizes his arguments with the words "Only God can know God", explained as "It is the God who is in the prophets who knows and reveals the God of the prophets. It is that same God who is in every person capable of knowing God in everything and in every man" [18].

---

[11] *Ab'ad min Mūskū wa min Washinṭun* (Far from Moscow and Washington), p. 51 f.

[12] "Man ẓalamak" (Who wronged you?), *al-Bayādir*, p. 55 : "God sees His Self in His Self, and He sees the Universe in its totality and says : "That is I". The Universe (*al-wuǧūd*) with everthing tangible and intangible in it is God's living body". *Cf.* "al-Fann al-akbar" (The Supreme Art), *al-Bayādir*, p. 69 : "In everything God created, He only created His Self".

[13] "Madrasat al-ǧamī'" (Everyman's School), *al-nūr wa al-dayǧūr*, p. 90 : "When will Man perceive that nature is the visible body of the invisible God".

[14] "Siḥr al-wuǧūd", (*al-Bayādir*, p. 36).

[15] "Naḥnu 'aḥsan 'am ābā'unā" (Are we better or our parents), *Ṣawt al-'ālam*, p. 134.

[16] *Kitāb Mirdād* (Arabic edition), p. 74. *The Book of Mirdad* (English edition), p. 43.

[17] "al-Dīn wa al-shabāb" (Religion and Youth), *Zād al-ma'ād*, p. 129.

[18] Op. cit., p. 130.

The idea that man is God in essence is also apparent in the frequently made reference to the Old Testament text that God created man in his image and likeness. Thus, in the essay "al-Nūr wa al-dayǧūr" (Light and Darkness) he writes : '... to elevate him until he becomes worthy of the inheritance that has been prepared for him since eternity — verily that is godliness. Has not it been said — and how true is it — that man is God's image and likeness?" [19]

Notwithstanding man's divine essence, an enormous gap must be bridged before this essence, according to Nuʿaymah, is reunited with its source. On the whole he is more concerned with overcoming this gap than indicating its cause, though he does offer a few explanations. The commonest cause in Nuʿaymah's writings is misunderstanding on the part of man. In the story "The Crow's Sermon", the crow says : "In the beginning which has no commencement there was 'I' and there was 'the world' and 'the world' was 'I' and 'I' was 'the world'. The two were inseparably and indivisibly one, and the one was beautiful and perfect. In the dawn of the first time a son was born to the earth and the son was called 'man'. 'Man' was beautiful and perfect; he was one with the world, until the world once asked him : 'Who are you' and he answered : 'I' — 'I'. The world asked 'Who am I' and he answered : 'You are the world'. At that moment man created suffering, because he divided his self into two parts. The one he called 'I' and the other 'World' " [20].

In an essay, probably written between 1932 and 1936, the Biblical story of man's fall from paradise is interpreted to a similar end. After having eaten the fatal apple, man arrived at the fallacious opinion that he was other than God [21]. This concept of delusion (*wahm*) as the cause of separation between man and God occurs in other places and in different contexts in Nuʿaymah's writings [22]. Its counterpart is knowledge which is the purpose of man's life [23].

Nuʿaymah returns to the story of man's fall from paradise to declare it the beginning

---

19 "al-Nūr wa al-dayǧūr" (Light and Darkness) in the volume of the same title, p. 15. Cf. also *al-Bayādir*, p. 56, 68; *Ṣawt al-ʿālam*, p. 19, 129, 148; *Fī mahabb al-rīḥ*, p. 108.

20 "ʿIẓat al-ghurāb" (The Sermon of the Crow), *al-Marāḥil*, p. 131. Cf. *The Book of Mirdad* (English Version), p. 38-40. *Kitāb Mirdād* (Arabic version), p. 64-70.

21 "Yanābīʿ al-alam" (The Sources of Pain), *Zād al-maʿād*, p. 62.

22 As in "Waǧh Yasūʿ" (The Face of Jesus), *al-Marāḥil*, p. 41 : "Does not Eve's and Adam's eating from the tree of 'the knowledge of good and evil' symbolize the beginning of the alertness of divine thought in its abode of clay? (*al-ǧibillah al-turābiyyah*). Is not the parental sin simply the fallacious idea that thought, bound to the clay, cannot live outside the clay".

23 *Zād al-maʿād*, p. 44; *Ṣawt al-ʿālam*, p. 33, 143; *al-Nūr wa al-dayǧūr*, p. 35; *Durūb*, p. 61. Cf. also the paradise story in "Madaniyyat al-ʿaql wa madaniyyat al-khayāl" (The Civilization of Reason and the Civilization of Imagination), *Ṣawt al-ʿālam*, p. 51. For the term *Khayāl* see p. 102 f. and footnotes 50 and 52.

of man's ascent to God. "It was the greatest and best venture upon which our parents in paradise entered, for they hazarded their lives to know God and to become Gods like Him" [24].

The image of the babe in swaddling-bands and the concept of man's delusion that he is other than God, are in the same line of thought. The metaphor of the beast in man which has to be curbed cannot be brought into that line. Contrary to the monistic concept of the world underlying the former statements the notion of a detracting force in man is based on dualism. Man is the center of two conflicting forces, according to Nu'aymah, "because the beast in him forces him down, and the God in him pushes him upwards" [25]. Evolutionism, again, is apparent in the statement that "man has not risen above the beast that part of him remain beast and part man, but to rise out above the beast and the man [26].

The ultimate destiny of man, according to Nu'aymah is to become God. Following the theosophical doctrine, he holds that man has to depend entirely on his own efforts except that he has been given all the time he needs to reach his destination, as well as the necessary provisions. Or, man is tied to the earth through an almost endless chain of rebirths, until he succeeds in breaking away from it all [27].

Much as Nu'aymah seems to have been impressed by the teachings of Mme Blavatsky's disciples, his approach to theosophy is as eclectic as the theosophists' towards religions and philosophies. The so-called intermediate period, or the time elapsing between death and rebirth of the same individual, so important to Mme Blavatsky, receives schant attention. "I do not want to speak extensively about life after death.

---

[24] "'Ālam ğunna ğunūnuhu" (A Mad World), *al-Nūr wa al-dayğūr*, p. 34. In *Ṣawt al-'ālam*, "Madaniyyat al-'aql wa madaniyyat al-khayāl", p. 50 ff. Nu'aymah makes use of the Biblical element that man was *misled* into eating the apple. *The Book of Mirdad* also carries the notion of a fall : "In his pathetic rush to cover up his *nakedness* Man has put on too many aprons which in the course of years have stuck so tightly to his skin that he no longer distinguishes between them and his skin. (English edition, p. 157, Arabic version, p. 275).

[25] "al-Nūr wa al-dayğūr" (Light and Darkness) in the volume of the same title, p. 15. Cf. "Fī mahabb al-rīḥ" (Windward), in the volume of the same title, p. 31 : "The essence of religion is to raise man from the plane of the beast (*bahīmah*) to the level of divinity". "al-Dīn wa al-madrasah (Religion and the School), *Fī mahabb al-rīḥ*, p. 67 : "... to curb the restiveness of the beast in his nature". "al-Midhwad wa al-ṣalīb" (The Manger and the Cross), *al-Nūr wa al-dayğūr*, p. 212 : "The birth of the Messiah in a place for cattle is but symbolizing the animal beginning of man".

[26] "al-Nūr wa al-dayğūr" (Light and Darkness), in the volume of the same title, p. 15.

[27] Nu'aymah alludes to or writes about reincarnation in "al-Ma'rifah wa al-madrasah" (Knowledge and the School), *Zād al-ma'ād*, p. 45; "Hal aflasa al-dīn" (Has Religion become Bankrupt), *al-Bayādir*, p. 116 f.; "Mihmāz al-baqā'" (The Urge to Survive), *Ṣawt al-'ālam*, p. 32 f. Other essays dealing with reincarnation are mentioned in the following footnotes relating to quotations in the text.

My point is not (*famā hammanī*) how the dead live nor where they live. The main thing I want to convey to your mind is that death is not the mournful end we imagine, and that it is no obstacle on man's road to his lofty goals" [28]. Nu'aymah once departs from this point of view in *The Book of Mirdad*: "What once occurred in Time is bound to re-occur again and again; the intervals, in the case of Man, may be long or brief, depending on the intensity of each man's desire and will for repetition" [29].

One of the earliest writings in which Nu'aymah speaks of reincarnation is a portrait entitled "The Face of Buddha". In this work he expresses his admiration for the spiritual elevation shining from Buddha's face. In a paraphrase of Buddha's teachings Nu'aymah writes : "Earthly life is a chastisement because it is a string of desires leading man from birth to death and from death to birth. The earth will exert its pulling force on everybody who clings to the earth, generation after generation. He will remain in the "whirlpool of births" until he cuts his earthly ties and makes his self escape from its delusions to let it merge with the "world self", where it will obtain Nirvana. Whoever wishes to liberate himself from the delusions of matter must kill every desire, every pleasure, and every wish, except the wish to reach Nirvana" [30].

In the volume *al-Bayādir* (The Threshing Floors) Nu'aymah rewords Buddha's teachings, showing his own conviction unambiguously. "If one life-time is not enough — and it will not be enough — for you to reach the goal — time is enough and to spare for countless lives. If the earth is not sufficient for you — and it will not be sufficient — in the expanse there are abodes in abundance" [31].

The essay "al-Mukhaddirāt al-ma'nawiyyah" (The Mental Drugs) seems to reflect the unbelief Nu'aymah encountered. He no longer propounds the doctrine of reincarnation, but instead tries to demonstrate its probability : "If sleep belongs to the most excellent and artful drugs in nature's pharmacy, then death is the out and out superior and ingenious one. The outward similarity between sleep and death almost carries us to the conclusion that they derive from one source, and that there is no difference other than the shorter or longer duration of the fainting spell. After we have been

[28] "al-Nūr wa al-dayǧūr" (Light and Darkness) in the volume of the same title, p. 20. *wa annahu lā yaqif fī sabīl al-insān* … .

[29] *The Book of Mirdad* (English edition), p. 97; *Kitāb Mirdād* (Arabic version), p. 166. Cf. also *The Book of Mirdad*, p. 90 : "All Time is lifetime, My Companions. There are no halts and starts in Time. Nor are there caravanserais where travellers may stop for refreshment and rest". (Arabic version, p. 156). According to Mme. Blavatsky, after each death the higher parts of the human ego fall into the devachanic state which is a state of bliss (*The Key to Theosophy*, p. 97 ff.). In her opinion the Nirvana includes a cyclic Rest, after which a new cycle of births and deaths begins (p. 102 f.).

[30] "Waǧh Būdhā" (The Face of Buddha), *al-Marāḥil*, p. 12.

[31] "al-Fann al-akbar" (The Supreme Art), *al-Bayādir*, p. 79.

drugged to sleep we recover from it to a new day after a few hours. How do we know that when we are benumbed by death we will not sober up again to a new life after some years?" [32]

In the novel *Liqā'* (Encounter) Leonardo tries to escape from the cycle of birth and death after he had made a vain attempt in a previous life. The novel relates the successful attempt, and how Leonardo prepares himself for it. It is remarkable that the goal is reached in a state of extasy in which music plays a major role, as it does in certain Ṣūfī practices [33]. Mirdād, the main character in *The Book of Mirdad*, is said to have led many lives. In the introductory chapter he is said to have been the helmsman aboard Noah's ark, visible to Noah alone. The story continues with Noah ordering his sons to build a monastery in the shape of the ark, and to form a community of nine persons in remembrance of those who sailed on the ark. In due time, Noah prophesies, the mysterious ninth man will return to save mankind from the fireflood. The core of the book is formed by the story of the returned Mirdād, whose conversations with a generation of monks long after Noah, were duly written down by one of his disciples in what is called *The Book of Mirdad* [34]. In a way Mirdād reminds of the Perfect Man of the Ṣūfīs, but he also fits in "the doctrine of Avatars, or divine incarnations, through which the teaching of the Mysteries is from time to time renewed and restored" [35]. Finally, Mirdād is not without parallels to Christ and to the gospel.

Sometimes Nu'aymah mentions a general human progress towards the ultimate goal. The theory of evolution, which seems at the back of this idea, is not unknown in theosophical doctrine, and seems not to have been considered incompatible with the idea of reaching the goal individually at intervals. In one of his essays Nu'aymah writes : "But history by connecting 'what we were' with 'what we are' makes it easy for us to see that mankind, notwithstanding the multitude of peoples nor the number of their roads, is one cavalcade travelling along one road towards one goal" [36]. The same idea is expressed by Nu'aymah when he explains that human progress is almost imperceptible, because "the speed of the caravan is measured against the speed of its slowest camel" [37].

---

[32] "al-Mukhaddirāt al-ma'nawiyyah" (The Mental Drugs), *al-Nūr wa al-dayǧūr*, p. 93.

[33] Cf. Ch. IV, p. 93.

[34] *Kitāb Mirdād*, p. 10 ff. *The Book of Mirdad* (English version), p. 9 ff.

[35] *Bhagavad Gita*. Translated with an introduction and commentary by Charles Johnston. Flushing, New York, 1908. p. xxviii of the commentary. For the Perfect Man, cf. the article of this title in R. A. Nicholson, *Studies in Islamic Mysticism*. Cambridge, 1921 (repr. 1967), p. 75-142. See p. 87, footnote 3 : "As in the pseudo-Clementine writings, Adam or Christ, the true prophet and perfect incarnation of the Divine spirit, is represented as manifesting himself personnally in a whole series of subsequent bearers of Revelation".

[36] "Ṣawt al-'ālam" (The Voice of the World), in the volume of the same title, p. 9.

[37] "Bashariyyah ǧadīdah" (A New Humanity), *al-Nūr wa al-dayǧūr*, p. 173.

The concept of continuing human progress can also be observed in Nu'aymah's assertion that "mankind will not regress to the animal, however much the fraud may counterfeit, the swindler may falsify..." [38]. Consider also this line : "A liability has been laid on his neck (*fī 'unuqihi amānah*). If this generation is blind to it, and fails to pay it back, the coming generations will not be blind to it nor fail to make a restitution" [39].

In one of his early essays, Nu'aymah professes something completely different from the belief in the ultimate unification of every human soul with the godhead. In the course of an argument about the Day of Judgment he writes : "Is not that day, the day of the separation of the sheep from the goats and the corn from the chaff, is it not the day on which your father will receive every spirit who has overcome the delusions of the body, and return to the earth, every spirit clinging to the earth, where there shall be weeping and gnashing of teeth, where the worm of yearning dieth not and the fire of desire is not quenched?" [40]. This opinion, however, stands isolated from Nu'aymah's other ideas about human destiny. His explanation of the Bible here does not seem to be in conformity with Greek Orthodox exegesis.

Important though these ideas may be, the central theme of Nu'aymah's writing is not the cycle of birth and death itself, but the requirements laid on man to live up to his destiny.

Nu'aymah opens the essay "Knowledge and the School" with the following words : "If you would ask me to define the purpose of man's life in a single word, I would say : 'Knowledge', and if you would ask what I mean by knowledge I would answer, 'Man's knowledge of the self'. For Man through his spirit is a world into which all seen and unseen worlds converge. They have no existence except in him, and when he knows what is in him, he knows all" [41]. Elsewhere he writes that the purpose of Man's existence is the knowledge of the self which means knowledge of God, which again means knowledge of all, and omniscience means omnipotence and freedom from every shackle and chain (*qayd wa ḥadd*) [42]. In yet another place Nu'aymah asserts that the "distant and most exalted goal is "omniscience, omnipotence and freedom which lead Man back to his divine source and make him God" [43].

---

[38] "al-Nur wa al-dayǧūr" (Light and Darkness), in the volume of that name, p. 27.

[39] *Op. cit.*, p. 30.

[40] The Biblical references are *St. Matthew* 25, 32; *St. Matthew* 24, 51 and *St. Marc* 9, 44. "Thalāthat wuǧūh, Waǧh Yasū'" (Three Faces, the Face of Jesus), *al-Marāḥil*, p. 44.

[41] "al-Ma'rifah wa al-madrasah" (Knowledge and the School), *Zād al ma'ād*, p. 44.

[42] "Qīmat al-insān" (The Value of Man), *Ṣawt al-'ālam*, p. 143 f.

[43] "Risālat al-sharq al-mutaǧaddid" (The Message of the Renovated East), *Durūb*, p. 61.

This knowledge, Nu'aymah makes clear, is completely different from what is gained in the schools and other institutes of learning [44]. He illustrates his point of view with the story of his encounter with a three-fold doctor searching for a God in whom to believe. Learning in this story is defined as trash in comparison to what Nu'aymah considers to be essential knowledge [45]. It is typical of his style that the three-fold doctor passes an unfavourable judgement over learning, and that Nu'aymah as his interlocutor does not even give a faint hint in that direction.

To attain this knowledge Man has been equiped with a set of instruments, which, according to Nu'aymah, guarantees Man that knowledge is both available and accessible for him. There are some variations in the set of instruments in the different essays, but the most frequently occurring set consists of "thought" (*fikr*), (*khayāl*) and "will" (*irādah*) [46]. The workings of the *khayāl*, meaning extra-sensory perception or imagination, is explained more than once. In an essay devoted to the *khayāl* Nu'aymah defines it as the ability "to see with banded eyes, to hear with sealed ears, to smell with a stuffed up nose..." [47].

In comparison to reason, Nu'aymah writes, "the *khayāl* is the sun which illuminates in a flash what ten thousands of lamps do not light in ten thousands of years. It is the magic ladder on which we climb from the sensory in us to the extra-sensory. Reason is but one of its rungs" [48]. Instead of reason being part of the *khayāl*, as it is in the quoted lines, Nu'aymah also discerns an ascending order in which the *khayāl* represents the higher, and reason the lower level : "When reason becomes elevated it is *khayāl*, and when *khayāl* descends it becomes reason" [48a]. The *khayāl*, moreover, is capable of growth, or at least in man's deployment of it, as Nu'aymah asserts in the following words : "As regards those the wings of whose *khayāl* have grown strong with long and steady pinions, to them I say : "Come on, release your *khayāl* from the cages of reason and fly with it where it flies with you..." " [49].

[44] "al-Ma'rifah wa al-madrasah" (Knowledge and the School), *Zād al-ma'ād*, p. 45.

[45] "Raghīf wa ibrīq mā'" (A Loaf and a Jug of Water), *al-Bayādir*, p. 187-193, esp. p. 191.

[46] "al-Nūr wa al-dayğūr" (Light and Darkness), in the volume of the same name, p. 15; the sequence is *fikr*, *wiğdān* and *khayāl*. Elsewhere in this volume the combination is *fikr*, *khayāl* and *irādah*. See pp. 109, 165 and 198. In the essay "Risālat al-sharq al-mutağaddid" (The Message of the Renovated East), *Durūb*, p. 63, the series counts four elements : *fikr*, *wiğdān*, *khayāl* and *irādah* and this same series with a small change in its order occurs in *Ab'ad min Mūskū wa min Washinṭun* (Far from Moscow and Washington), p. 37 : *Fikr*, *khayāl*, *wiğdān* and *irādah*. Nu'aymah himself translates *khayāl* as "imagination". Cf. *The Book of Mirdad*, p. 151 : "It has unloosed your imagination from the grip of the despotic senses". Arabic version in *Kitāb Mirdād*, p. 263.

[47] "al-Khayāl", *Zād al-ma'ād*, p. 9.

[48] Madiniyyat al-'aql wa madaniyyat al-khayāl" (The Civilization of Reason and the Civilization of Imagination), *Ṣawt al-'ālam*, p. 50. Cf. also the essay "al-Khayāl", *Zād al-ma'ād*, p. 7-19.

[48a] "Ğanāḥā al-bashariyyah" (The Two Wings of Humanity), *Zād al-ma'ād*, p. 75.

[49] "al-Khayāl", *Zād al-ma'ād*, p. 13.

Nu'aymah's use of the word *khayāl*, however, is not limited to the meanings given above. On the one hand the *khayāl* is divine [50], but on the other hand it is also used to mean "reflection" or "shadow". In one essay Nu'aymah writes about the *khayāl* of a pyramid in the water [51], and in his autobiography he relates that he and his schoolfriends once tried to step on each other's *khayāl* cast by the rising sun [52]. Last not least, the *khayāl* together with logic, reason and the will, is mentioned as a cause of corruption as far as Man's utterances are concerned [53].

In some of Nu'aymah's writings the *baṣīrah* (vision), as distinguished from the *baṣar* (eye-sight), has about the same function as the *khayāl* [54].

The "will" (*Irādah*) is another instrument Man has at his disposal. With it, Nu'aymah writes, Man has to defend and to uphold the values he is able to create through his thought and his *khayāl* [55]. In Nu'aymah's reasoning this vindication of values amounts to Man's voluntary conformation to the world order. The alternative is that Man is forced to obey, and thus is limited in his freedom [56]. Unlike the *khayāl*, which is linked to the supreme *khayāl*, Nu'aymah discerns a complete hierarchy with regard to the will : "Because above the will of any man and any people is the will of all humanity, and over the will of humanity is the will of the earth on the flesh and blood

50 "Madaniyyat al-'aql wa madaniyyat al-khayāl" (The Civilization of Reason and the Civilization of Imagination), *Ṣawt al-'ālam*, p. 51 : "Except that she did not become aware of the God in her — that is her *khayāl* — until she perceived together with it her human nature, and that is her reason ('aql)", p. 54 : God is *khayāl muğarrad muṭlaq* (absolute unique *khayāl*). Cf. "al-Madhāhib wa al-mutamadhhibūn" (Doctrines and Doctrinaires), *al-Bayādir*, p. 22 : "al-khayāl al-akbar" (The supreme *khayāl*), in contrast to a wandering *khayāl*. On p. 21 occurs the opposition "lower" and "higher" *khayāl*.

51 "al-Fann al-akbar" (The Supreme Art), *al-Bayādir*, p. 73.

52 "al-Muwağğih al-a'ẓam" (The Supreme Director), *al-Nūr wa al-dayğur*, p. 130. *Khayāl*, in the sense of "shadow" or "spectre", is also used in connection with abstracts : *al-Nās la ya'rifūn min al-ḥurriyyah ḥata khayālahu* (People do not even know the shadow of freedom), "al-Abwāq al-muḥaṭṭamah" (The broken Trumpets), *Zād al-ma'ād*, p. 24; *khayāl al-taqālīd al-'aqīm* (The Sterile Spectre of Traditions); "Ḍabāb al-taqālīd" (The Mists of Traditions), *Zād al-ma'ād*, p. 119.

53 "Māhiyyat al-adab wa muhimmatuhu" (The Essence and Importance of Literature), *Durūb*, p. 37 : Deceit, hypocrisy and pretence have nothing to do, Nu'aymah writes, with spontaneous utterance. "It always is the truth and the very truth, contrary to the utterance in which logic, reason, the *khayāl* and the will have a large share".

54 "al-Taw'amān : al-Sharq wa al-gharb" (The Twins : The East and the West), the first part of this essay is entitled : "Sharq baṣīr wa gharb mubṣir" (A Visionary East and a Seeing West), *al-Bayādir*, p. 136 ff.

55 "Fī mawkib al-tağaddud" (In the Trail of Renovation), *al-Nūr wa al-dayğūr*, p. 166.

56 "Bashariyyah ğadīdah" (A New Mankind), *al-Nūr wa al-dayğūr*, p. 171 f. Cf. also *Ab'ad min Mūskū wa min Washinṭun* (Far from Moscow and Washington), p. 47.

of which humanity is feeding, and over the will of the earth is the will of the universe (*maskūnah*) of the gigantic body of which the earth is but a tiny member" [56a].

Behind all this is an irrational force, escaping human control, described by Nu'aymah as being comparable to the instinct of the animal, or likened to thirst and hunger and named "desire" or "longing" [57].

As regards the consequences of unwillingness or misbehaviour, Nu'aymah follows the theosophical law of retribution, which stipulates that a man's deed will return to himself sooner or later. The "later" in theosophical doctrine commonly means a following life of the same man. In Nu'aymah's writings the notion of suffering in the present life being caused by deeds in a previous life occurs only once. The main character of the novel *al-Yawm al-akhīr* (The last Day) thinks about the man born blind, and the question of the disciples of Jesus, if the man himself or his parents had sinned because he has been born blind. In the end he concludes that the child and his parents have transgressed "God's will" in a former life [58].

Nu'aymah may have been Biblically inspired also when he wrote : "The blood we spill, the bone we break, the child we orphanize, the house we destroy over its inhabitants, is blood we shall be forced one day to compensate for with our blood, and a bone we shall be driven to restore with our bones, and a child we shall be held responsible for its being an orphan, and a house we shall be compelled to re-erect from the stones of our house" [59]. Nu'aymah's concern, however, is not with the sin committed in a former life, or the pains awaiting Man in a following life, but Man's present condition and its causes. "The pains, of whatever kind they are, which overcome you alone, are the outcome of the thoughts, actions and desires of you alone" [60]. The cure for all the ills that befall Man is, as we have seen, obedience to God, or, to the world order.

[56a] "al-Muwağğih al-a'ẓam" (The Supreme Director), *al-Nūr wa al-dayğūr*, p. 123.

[57] "al-Nūr wa al-dayğūr" (Light and Darkness) in the volume of the same name, p. 16 : As Life has armed the animal with the instinct by which it is led to its food, its drink, its place of shelter and to the animals of its kind, so life has armed the human heart with desires by which it is led to its goals. Thereafter it has armed him with thought and imagination... (*fikr* and *khayāl*). "Mihmāz al-baqā'" (The Spur to Survival), *Ṣawt al-'ālam*, p. 30 : "Hunger and its twin-brother thirst continually push us to go and to move". Modern psychology may have helped Nu'aymah to find the following explanation : "Uneasiness is our perception of being disturbed (*huwa shu'ūrunā bi al-inzi'āğ min ḥālah naḥnu fīhā*). This uneasiness generates in us a desire to get rid of what disturbs us, and the desire in its turn, generates a current of thought and action". *Ab'ad min Mūskū wa min Washinṭun* (Far from Moscow and Washington), p. 13.

[58] *al-Yawm al-akhīr* (The Last Day), pp. 150 ff., esp. p. 155.

[59] "Ilā ayn" (Where are we going?), *Ṣawt al-'ālam*, p. 175.

[60] "al-Ḥuzn wa al-ḥazānā" (Sadness and the Sad), *Ṣawt al-'ālam*, p. 196.

The conviction that man is the ultimate cause of his own well-being or affliction did not hinder Nuʿaymah from expressing his belief in the direct interference in life of a providential agency, the "supreme director" or "the unseen hand". In the essay "The Supreme Director" he relates a number of incidents which he believes to have been moved by a force outside himself. To these workings of an exterior agent he counts the establishment of a Russian school in Biskintā; the unexpected return of his brother from the U.S.A. in 1911, which made him pursue his studies in Seattle instead of in Paris; and the incident of the rucksack which he retrieved in one try from among hundreds of rucksacks in the dead of the night in wartime France in 1918. About this last event Nuʿaymah tells us that on his way to the pile of rucksacks the thought occurred to him that he would come out of the war unhurt if the first rucksack he picked up would be his own [61].

A large part of Nuʿaymah's writings deal with human inter-relationships, such as the relation between individuals regardless of sex, the relation between men and women, and mondial relationships. In Nuʿaymah's system these interhuman rapports, it seems justified to assume, function within his concept of the absolute unity of Man. What this unity amounts to is explained in the essay "Anta al-Insāniyyah" (You are mankind), which opens with the following lines : "You are mankind in its entirety. You are its A and its Z (*Alifuhā wa yā'uhā*). From you spring its sources; they return to you and pour into you. You are its ruler and its ruled, its tyrant and its oppressed, its destructor and what is destroyed" [62].
Words to the same meaning occur in the essay "Gharb ḥākim wa sharq maḥkūm" (A ruling West and a ruled East) : "One of the figments — how many they are — besetting man's brains is that one man can rule another man without being ruled by him. The fact is that no relation between one creature and another exists without both of them having a share in it, and without the portion of the one being equal to that of the other" [63]. The interdependence of all earthly beings is poignantly expressed by Mirdād in two rhetorical questions and their answers : "Is not a donkey driver led by his donkey's tail? Is not a jailer bound unto the jailed? Verily the donkey drives his leader; the jailbird jails his jailer" [64].

The idea of the unity of mankind and the concept of equality in human relations have hardly a share in Nuʿaymah's discourses on poverty. Human unity is scarce reflected in : "We all are hungry, thirsty and naked. By what logic do we fight each other instead of being one army, one will and one weapon in our fight against hunger,

---

61 "al-Muwağğih al-aʿẓam" (The Supreme Director), *al-Nūr wa al-dayğūr*, p. 121-146.
62 "Anta al-insāniyyah" (You are Mankind), *al-Marāḥil*, p. 91.
63 "Gharb ḥākim wa sharq maḥkūm" (A Ruling West and a Ruled East), *al-Bayādir*, p. 153.
64 *Kitāb Mirdād* (Arabic version), p. 287. *The Book of Mirdad* (English edition), p. 164.

thirst and nakedness". The equality of shares in human relations shines through in the sentence : "As long as there is one pauper among men they all are poor". But here Nuʿaymah makes a shift from material to spiritual poverty [65].

On the whole Nuʿaymah has little to say about poverty, probably because in his eyes it was a minor problem. He devoted only one essay to it plus some random remarks in other writings [66].

Nuʿaymah knows of various causes of poverty in the Arab countries. There is, however, some oddity in that he at one time lays the blame on the colonizing countries [67], and at another on the Arabs themselves [68]. They had by causing the poverty prepared a fertile soil for colonialism. In general, however, the rich are to blame : "Nobody sleeps on an empty stomach but for the reason that somebody else eats or hoards in excess of his needs from the goods of earth and of heaven. Nobody is in want of a coat for any other reason than that his neighbour has two... The gluttony of the surfeited is the cause of the hunger of the starving. From the gracefulness of the elegant springs the nakedness of the destitute" [69].

Nuʿaymah states in the same essay that if a complete and precise account were made out, the beneficiary probably would have a claim on his well-doer to a multiple amount of the alms bestowed on him [70].

His preaching, however, is not without its bourgeois leanings when he declares that the 'magnanimous, when he possesses some knowledge, fortune and power, does not boast of it before the unlearned, the poor and the powerless. On the contrary, he belittles the value of these things for fear that the unlearned, the poor and the powerless become embarrassed (*yakhğal minhu*) [71].

Nuʿaymah devotes some attention to the status of women, without, however, showing the slightest admiration for feminist activities. He declares that the movement is based on a fallacy, "that the man is free and the woman a slave, and that he has more from life than she has, that he is strong and she weak..." [72]. "If she is a slave

[65] "Fuqarā'" (Poor), *Ṣawt al-ʿālam*, p. 203.

[66] "Fuqarā'", *Ṣawt al-ʿālam*, pp. 199-206. Cf. "Lubnān" (Lebanon), *al-Nūr wa al-dayğūr*, p. 105 : "When you wander through the mountain villages you will be amazed not to find Lebanese beggars".

[67] "Ghāndī — Damīr al-sharq al-mustayqiẓ" (Ghandi — the Conscience of the Awakened East), *Fī mahabb al-rīḥ*, p. 114.

[68] "Ḥulāfā' al-istiʿmār" (The Allies of Colonialism), *Durūb*, p. 158.

[69] "Fuqarā'" (Poor), *Ṣawt al-ʿālam*, p. 202 f.

[70] "Fuqarā'" (Poor), *Ṣawt al-ʿālam*, p. 202.

[71] "Ṣighār al-nufūs wa kibāruhā" (Small-minded and magnanimous people), *Durūb*, p. 78 f.

[72] "Muthallith al-ḥayāh" (The Triangle of Life). *al-Marāḥil*, p. 101.

it is because the man is a slave, or if the man is a slave it is because she is a slave..." [73]. He repeats this point of view in "The man does not enslave the woman without making himself a slave before he enslaves her" [74].

Similar ideas occur in his address to the pupils of a school for girls in Homs in 1933 : "And now, if you should ask my opinion on what is called 'the freedom of women' and on the tremendous efforts spent for its sake, I would answer that it is founded on a fallacy. That fallacy is that the man is free and the woman enslaved. They both are, in my opinion, as long as the one is bound by the other, free through the freedom of the partner and slave through his slavery" [75].

In his later writings Nuʿaymah has tried to fit the relationship between men and women into his theory about the return to God and the necessary acquisition of knowledge. The splitting of men into male and female was indispensable if man were to gain knowledge, according to Nuʿaymah : "Adam before he had Eve, was in a state of blissful ignorance resembling that of infancy, having no thought, no power, no will. The tree of good and evil and the tree of life were within his reach, but he did not stretch his hand to them. After he had become two, however, the first thing he sensed in himself was his longing for knowledge, and there is no knowledge without comparison, and comparison does not exist except between two dissimilar things. Adam was split in his self to gain knowledge of his self. The road of good and evil is the only road to knowledge" [76].

Sexuality is thus translated into a drive for knowledge. In *Mudhakkarāt al-Arqash* the frustration of this drive brings al-Arqash to slaughter his wife [77]. Leonardo, in *Liqā'*, on the other hand, is pictured as successful and as undoing the duality of male and female. Why this involves the end of his and his fiancee's earthly existence is not properly explained [78].

---

73 "Muthallith al-ḥayāh" (The Triangle of Life), *al-Marāḥil*, p. 102.

74 *loc. cit.*

75 "Ǧanāḥā al-bashariyyah" (The Two Wings of Humanity), *Zād al-maʿād*, p. 76.

76 "Umm al-ḥayāh" (The Mother of Life), *Fī mahabb al-rīḥ*, p. 108 f. Cf. "Māhiyyat al-adab wa muhimmatuhu" (The Essence and Importance of Literature), *Durūb*, p. 50 : "Man was not split into two to be male and female except to cut the stretch of duality, the stretch of good and evil — and so to gain knowledge of himself, and to be reunited again in the perfect man who is neither male nor female". See also "Lughz al-mar'ah" (The Enigma of the Female), *al-Nūr wa al-dayǧūr*, p. 80 f. Esp. p. 81 : "As regards procreation, which appears to us as if it were the first and last goal of the existence of women, verily that is nothing but a powerful incentive for men and women together in their search for knowledge". Cf. also *The Book of Mirdad* (English edition), p. 180, *Kitāb Mirdād* (Arabic version), p. 318.

77 See Ch. IV, p. 50 f.

78 See Ch. IV, p. 51 f.

The subject is also treated in the *Book of Mirdad* by Mirdād, who among other things has the following to teach : "And what are man and woman but the single Man unconscious of his singleness and so cloven in twain and made to quaff the gall of Duality that he may yearn for the nectar of Unity... Let men and women, who are yet not far from the stallion and the mare, and from the buck and the doe, seek each other in the dark seclusions of the flesh... But men and women yearners must realize their unity even while in the flesh, not by communion of the flesh, but by the Will to Freedom of the flesh and all the impediments it places in their way to perfect Unity and Holy Understanding" [79]. Nu'aymah defines the drive of Man towards this unity of man and woman as love . But in order to distinguish it from sexual love, he uses the word *maḥabbah* instead of *ḥubb* [80]. *Maḥabbah* in Nu'aymah's writings also means the force which holds the universe together [81], reminding us of Plato's ἐρως.

When Nu'aymah deals with the relation of peoples his perspective changes. Instead of admonishing the stronger party as he did in his essays on poverty, or on the relations between men and women, he now directs his words to the weaker party, whose ego was hurt by foreign domination; by the Palestine issue; and by its technical and economic inadequacy in relation to Western countries. Most of his maxims about the ruler and the ruled, the master and the slave etc. are to be found in the context of his discussions of the relations between peoples [82]. He pursues the idea of equality by stressing that all mankind collaborated to make Man reach his present state of development [83] or, what amounts to the same, that all peoples have contributed something to the development of civilization [84]. Most of his efforts, however, are spent on underlining the role of the East in the genesis of Western civilization [85]. Among the writings Nu'aymah devoted to the relation between East and West is one

---

[79] *The Book of Mirdad* (English version), p. 106. *Kitāb Mirdād* (Arabic version), p. 181 f.

[80] "Lughz al-mar'ah" (The Enigma of the Female), *al-Nūr wa al-dayğūr*, p. 82.

[81] "Dustūr al-ṭabī'ah" (The Law of Nature), *Zād al-ma'ād*, p. 95. Cf. *The Book of Mirdad* (English version), p. 62 : "Love is the Law of God". *Kitāb Mirdād* (Arabic version), p. 108. Cf. also *The Book of Mirdad* (English edition), p. 65 : "This huge and ponderous mass of earth and rocks which you call Altar Peak would quickly fly asunder were it not held together by the hand of love". Arabic translation in *Kitāb Mirdād*, p. 113.

[82] See above p. 105.

[83] "Ilā ayn" (Where are we going?), *Ṣawt al-'ālam*, p. 163 f.

[84] "Risālat al-'ālam al-'arabī" (The Message of the Arab World), *Ṣawt al-'ālam*, p. 117 f. Nu'aymah warns the Arabs not to be proud of past or future achievements because all mankind has a share in them.

[85] "Ḥikāyat al-sharq wa al-gharb" (The Story of the East and the West), *Ṣawt al-'ālam*, p. 160. Cf. also "Nahḍat al-sharq al-'arabī" (The Resurgence of the Arab East), *al-Marāḥil*, p. 60 : "If you would take from Western civilization what it has borrowed from the East you would leave it a sepulchre adorned with gold on the outside but on the inside full of bones and worms".

long essay. Its main points are : that the West is materialistic and the East spiritual; that the East is called upon to shoulder anew the task of the spiritual leader of the world; and that the Western culture is on the wane [86].

Nu'aymah had already presaged the end of the Western civilization during his stay in the U.S.A. [87]. In his later writings the idea of a dying Western civilization [88] sometimes counterbalanced by a rising East has gained a firm foothold. Thus he could write that "the time in which we live perhaps is the end of those times..." [89] i.e. the time in which the lead of the material eye, meaning the West, is replaced by that of the inner eye characterizing the East. Elsewhere he likens the East and the West to a pair of scales. If one side rises the other goes down. "Times have gone past us in which the hand of the East went down and the hand of the West rose. Times in which the movement of the hands is reversed will not be long in following" [90].

The same thought, but generalized, is voiced by Nu'aymah when he asserts that power is unstable, and that the rulers of today may be the ruled of tomorrow [91]. The idea that the ruler is ruled by the ruled, does not seem to function here.

On the other hand, Nu'aymah seems to be well aware of the fact that his equation of the West with rationalism and of the East with spiritualism does not obtain in the actual situation of the moment. This awareness shimmers through in statements in which he refrains from differentiating between Eastern and Western civilization, but instead argues that the present civilization is coming to its end, and that a different sort of civilization is bound to replace it [92].

Nu'aymah's belief in a coming spiritual civilization has its bearing on the comments he wrote on Lebanese and Arab political issues. His approach towards such questions

---

[86] "al-Taw'amān : al-sharq wa al-gharb" (The Twinbrothers : The East and the West), *al-Bayādir*, p. 136-169. It may suffice here to quote the sub-headings of the successive parts of this essay : "The Visionary East and the Seeing West", p. 136-144; "The East Sets the Targets and the West Prepares (Levels) the Roads towards Them", p. 144-152; "The Ruling West and the Ruled East", p. 153-160; "The Waning West and the Rising East", p. 160-169.

[87] "Nahḍat al-sharq al-'arabī" (The Resurgence of the Arab East), *al-Marāḥil*, p. 62 f.

[88] "Madaniyyat al-ālāt wa al-azmāt" (The Civilization of Tools and Crises), *Zād al-ma'ād*, p. 39.

[89] "al-Taw'amān : al-sharq wa al-gharb" (The Twinbrothers : The East and The West), *al-Bayādir*, p. 139.

[90] "Ḥikāyat al-sharq wa al-gharb" (The Story of the East and The West), *Ṣawt al-'ālam*, p. 161.

[91] "al-Taw'amān : al-sharq wa al-gharb" (The Twinbrothers : The East and The West), *al-Bayādir*, p. 154.

[92] "al-Hadm wa al-binā'" (Destruction and Construction), *al-Bayādir*, p. 42. "Ilā ayn?" (Where are we going?), *Ṣawt al-'ālam*, p. 179; "Bashā'ir al-rabī'" (The Harbingers of Spring), *al-Nūr wa al-dayǧūr*, p. 57 f.

as Lebanese independence, and the Palestine issue, remind us of his attitude towards the women's movement, whose goals he declared to be based on a fallacy. The newly won independence of Lebanon elicited his comment as follows : "Oh, that independence where what they fancy it to be. Oh, that it were more than the replacement of one authority by another, a face by a face and a tongue by a tongue; Oh, that it were possible to obtain it — as they say — through the spending of money and blood. There would be no good more precious man could buy at such a paltry price.

But independence is different from what they say. Nobody is independent as long as there are pimples and ulcers of rancour in his heart and darkness upon darkness of fears in his thought. Nobody is independent as long as the penny is his master and sovereign (*amīr*), nor anybody whose reins are in the hand of somebody else" [93].

The Palestine question, Nuʿaymah argues, has not been created through a fault of the Jews, the Arabs or the Western powers, but by the whole world. The fundamental question, he asserts, is that of compatriot and foreigner [94]. Without this distinction the issue would never have arisen. Elsewhere he pleads for the abolition of borders and travel limitations, which are, in his opinion, incompatible with human dignity and with the unity of the world [95]. Once or twice Nuʿaymah resorts to fierce words on the Palestine issue, as in *Abʿad min Mūskū wa min Washinṭun* (Far from Moscow and Washinton) : "Therefore the Jews were dispersed in all the directions of the inhabited world, and there will be no new state for them as long as they build it on the same principles as their ancient state... every country that bought its existence and its might with the blood and the humiliation of others or with deceit, oppression, wealth and shrewdness will collapse" [96].

Most of Nuʿaymah's efforts go into inciting the East, or at least the Arabs, to become the spiritual leaders of the world, and to lead mankind to a new civilization based on belief, love and peace : "... the world is in need of a new leaven... Who is more worthy than we to offer that leaven to the world. Who is more worthy than this East to renew the message which radiated from its heart and its imagination (*khayāl*) over the world" [97]. The same idea occurs in the long essay he wrote about the twin-

---

93 "al-Taw'amān : al-sharq wa al-gharb" (The Twinbrothers : The East and The West), ***al-Bayādir***, p. 156. Cf. also "Qālū istaqalla Lubnān" (Lebanon has become Independent, they say), ***al-Bayādir***, p. 209-216.

94 "Mushkilat al-mashākil" (The Main Problem), *al-Nūr wa al-dayğūr*, p. 152.

95 Cf. *al-Bayādir*, pp. 49, 239; *Ṣawt al-ʿālam*, p. 15 ff., *al-Nūr wa al-dayğūr*, p. 174 ff.; *Abʿad min Mūskū wa min Washinṭun* (Far from Moscow and Washington), p. 58 ff.

96 *Abʿad min Mūskū wa min Washinṭun* (Far from Moscow and Washington), p. 58. *Cf. Sabʿūn* II, 133 and above p. 139 f.

97 "ʿInda al-shadā'id" (Concerning the Acts of Violence), *al-Nūr wa al-dayğūr*, p. 117 f.

brothers, the East and the West : "This mankind that has been bled by the lance of hatred and greed is in need of an encouraging voice to spare its clean blood, and to keep what has remained of it for nobler and loftier purposes than the substitution of rulers by rulers, borders by borders and plagues by plagues.

That voice shall come forth from the East — from this East which today is stupified by the sky-high summits in the heights of its soul and by the profundity of its depths" [98].

It cannot be doubted that Nu'aymah's foremost aim has been to formulate the message, which, according to him, the East had to offer the world. If any of his books should contain this message it must be sought in *The Book of Mirdad*, which he declares to be the peak of his intellectual achievement [99]. Under the weight of this spiritual mission the literary one had to recede, thus setting limits to the role he had so enthusiastically adopted during his stay in the U.S.A..

---

[98] "al-Taw'amān : al-sharq wa al-gharb" (The Twinbrothers : The East and The West), *al-Bayādir*, p. 158. Cf. "Ṣawt al-'ālam" (The Voice of the World), in the volume of the same title, p. 27 : "I want ... to see the East ... again carry the message of belief to the world". Cf. also "Risālat al-sharq al-mutağaddid" (The Message of the Renovated East), *Durūb*, p. 61. "al-Nūr wa al-dayğūr" (Light and Darkness) in the volume of the same title, p. 30.

[99] *Sab'ūn* III, p. 213.

BIBLIOGRAPHY

It has not been possible to present a complete bibliography of Mīkhā'īl Nu'aymah. Some editions of a few of his works were not traced in one of the public or University Libraries in Cairo and Beirut, in the bookshops or at the publishers, not withstanding the generous help that was offered.

The decision to mention the publishers' together with the place and date was taken after much of the relevant information had been gathered. It was physically impossible at that moment to retrace all the editions which had been listed already. The inevitable result is that the name of the publishers' could not be given for all editions.

Bibliographical information, such as place, publishers' and date not given on the title-page, has been placed between brackets.

First editions of works by Mīkhā'īl Nu'aymah
arranged after year of appearance

al-Ābā' wa al-banūn. New York, Sharikat al-Funūn, 1917.
al-Ghirbāl. Cairo, al-Maṭba'ah al-'aṣriyyah, 1923.
al-Marāḥil. Beirut, Maṭba'at Ṣādir, 1933.
Ğibrān Khalīl Ğibrān. Beirut, 1934.
Zād al-ma'ād. Cairo, Dār al-Muqtaṭaf wa al-Muqaṭṭam, 1936.
Kān mā kān. Beirut, Maṭba'at al-Ittiḥād, 1937.
al-Awthān. Beirut, Maktabat Ṣādir, 1946.
Karam 'alā darb. Cairo, Dār al-Ma'ārif, 1946.
Liqā'. Beirut, Maktabat Ṣādir, 1946.
The Book of Mirdad. Beirut, Sader's Library, 1948.
Ṣawt al-'Ālam. Cairo, Dār al-Ma'ārif, [1948?].
Mudhakkarāt al-Arqash. Beirut, Maktabat Ṣādir, 1949.
Gibran Kahlil Gibran (English edition). New York, The Philosophical Library, 1950.
al-Nūr wa al-dayğūr. Beirut, Dār Ṣādir, 1950.
Kitāb Mirdād. Beirut, Maṭba'at al-Manāhil, [1952].
Fī mahabb al-rīḥ. Beirut, Ṣādir, [1953].
Durūb. Beirut, Dār al-'ilm li al-malāyīn, 1954.
Akābir. Beirut, Dār Ṣādir, Dār Bayrūt, 1956.
Ab'ad min Mūskū wa min Washinṭun. Beirut, Dār Ṣādir, Dār Bayrūt, 1957.
Abū Baṭṭah. Beirut, Ṣādir, [1959].
Sab'ūn (3 vols.). Beirut, Dār Ṣādir, Dār Bayrūt, 1959-1960.
al-Yawm al-akhīr. Beirut, Dār Ṣādir, Dār Bayrūt, 1963.
Hawāmish. Beirut, Dār Ṣādir, Dār Bayrūt, 1965.
'Ayyūb. Beirut, Dār Ṣādir, [1967].
Yā Ibn Ādam! Beirut, Dār Ṣādir, [1969].
Fī al-ghirbāl al-ğadīd. Beirut, Mu'assasat Nawfal, 1972.
Aḥādīth ma' al-ṣiḥāfah. Beirut, Mu'assasat A. Badrān wa Shurakāhu, [1973].
Maqālāt mutafarriqah = al-Mağmū'ah al-kāmilah, vol. 7, pp. 122-364. Beirut, Dār al-'ilm li al-malāyīn, 1973.
Nağwā al-ghurūb. Beirut, Mu'assasat Nawfal, [1973].
Rasā'il = al-Mağmū'ah al-kāmilah, vol. 8. Beirut, Dār al-'ilm li al-malāyīn, 1974.
al-Mağmū'ah al-kāmilah, (Complete works) 8 vols. Beirut, Dār al-'ilm li al-malāyīn, 1970-1974

Bibliography of Arabic works by Mīkhā'il Nu'aymah

Al-Ābā' wa al-banūn. New York, Sharikat al-Funūn, 1917.
Second improved edition. Beirut, Maktab Sādir, [1953].
Third edition. Beirut, Dār Ṣādir [1959].
Fourth edition. Beirut, Dar Ṣādir, Dār Bayrūt, 1962.
Fifth edition. Beirut, Dār Ṣādir, [1967].
Sixth edition. Beirut, Mu'assasat Nawfal, [1971].
al-Mağmū'ah al-kāmilah (The Complete Works).
Vol. 4. Dār al-'ilm li al-malāyīn, 1971.

Ab'ad min Mūskū wa min Washinṭun. Beirut, Dār Ṣādir, Dār Bayrūt, 1957.
Second edition. Beirut, Dār Ṣādir, Dār Bayrūt, 1961.
Third edition. Bairut, Dār Ṣādir, [1966].
al-Mağmū'ah al-kāmilah. Vol. 6. Beirut, Dār al-'ilm li al-malāyīn, 1972.

Abū Baṭṭah.
First edition. Beirut, Ṣādir, [1959].
Second edition. Beirut, Dār Ṣādir, Dār Bayrūt, 1963.
Third edition. Beirut, Dār Ṣādir, [1966].
Fourth edition. Beirut, Mu'assasat Nawfal, [1971].
al-Mağmū'ah al-kāmilah. volume 2. Beirut, Dār al-'ilm li al-malāyīn, 1970.

Aḥādīth ma' al-ṣiḥāfah.
First edition. Beirut, Mu'assasat A. Badrān wa Shurakāhu, (1973).

Akābir.
First edition. Beirut, Dār Ṣādir, Dār Bayrūt, 1956.
Second edition. Beirut, Dār Ṣādir, Dār Bayrūt, 1963.
Third edition. Beirut, Dār Ṣādir, [1966].
Fourth edition. Beirut, Dār Ṣādir, [1967].
Fifth edition. Beirut, Mu'assasat Nawfal, [1972].
al-Mağmū'ah al-kāmilah. Vol. 2. Beirut, Dār al-'ilm li al-malāyīn, 1971.

al-Awthān.
First edition. Beirut, Maktabat Ṣādir, 1946.
Second(?) edition not traced.
Third (?) edition. Beirut, Dār Ṣādir, Dār Bayrūt, 1958.
Fourth edition. Beirut, Dār Ṣādir, Dār Bayrūt, 1962.
Fifth edition. Beirut, Dār Ṣādir, (1966).
Sixth edition not traced.
Seventh edition. Bairut, Mu'assasat Nawfal, (1971).
al-Magmū'ah al-kāmilah. vol. 6. Beirut, 1971.

Ayyūb.
First edition. Beirut, Dār Ṣādir, (1967).
al-Mağmū'ah al-kāmilah. vol. 4. Beirut, 1971.

al-Bayādir.
First edition. Cairo. Dār al-Ma'ārif, [1945].
Second edition not traced.
Third edition. Beirut, Dār Ṣādir, [1956].
Fourth edition. Beirut, Dār Ṣādir [1960].
Fifth edition. Beirut, Dār Ṣādir, Dār Bayrūt, 1963.
Sixth edition. Beirut, Dār Ṣādir, Dār Bayrūt, 1966.
Seventh edition. Beirut, Mu'assasat Nawfal, n.d.
al-Mağmū'ah al-kamilah, Vol. 4. Beirut, 1971.

Book of Murdad.

Durūb.
First edition. Beirut, Dār al-'ilm li al-malāyīn, 1954.
Second, revised and augmented edition. Beirut, Dār Ṣādir, Dār Bayrūt, 1960.
Third edition. Beirut, Dār Ṣādir, Dār Bayrūt, 1963.
Fourth edition. Beirut, Dār Ṣādir, Dār Bayrūt, 1966.
Fifth edition. Beirut, Dār Ṣādir, [1968].
Fifth (!) edition. Beirut, Mu'assasat Nawfal, [1971].
al-Mağmū'ah al-kāmilah. Vol. 6. Beirut, 1972.

Fī mahabb al-rīḥ.
First edition. Beirut, Ṣādir [1953].
Second edition. Beirut, Dār Ṣādir, Dār Bayrūt [1959].
Third edition. Beirut, Dār Ṣādir, Dār Bayrūt, 1962.
Fourth edition. Beirut, Dār Ṣādir, [1966].
Fifth edition. Beirut, Mu'assasat Nawfal, (1972).
al-Mağmū'ah al-kāmilah. Vol. 5. Beirut, 1971.

Fī al-ghirbāl al-ğadīd.
First edition. Beirut, Mu'assasat Nawfal, 1972.
al-Mağmū'ah al-kāmilah. Vol. 7. Beirut, 1973.

al-Ghirbāl.
First edition. Cairo, al-Maṭba'ah al-'aṣriyyah, 1923.
Second edition (?). Cairo, Dār al-Ma'ārif, 1946.
Third edition not traced.
Fourth edition. Cairo, Dār al-Ma'ārif, 1951.
Fifth edition. Cairo, Dār al-Ma'ārif, [1957].
Sixth edition. Beirut, Dār Ṣādir, Dār Bayrūt, 1960.
Seventh edition. Beirut, Dār Ṣādir, Dār Bayrūt, 1964.
Eighth edition not traced.
Ninth edition. Beirut, Mu'assasat Nawfal, 1971.
Al-Mağmū'ah al-kāmilah. Vol. 3. Beirut, 1971.

Ğibrān Khalīl Ğibrān.
First edition. Beirut, 1934 (not traced).
Second edition Beirut, Maktabat Ṣādir, 1943.
Third edition. Beirut, Maktabat Ṣādir, 1951.
Fourth edition. Beirut, Dār Ṣādir, Dār Bayrūt, 1960.
Fifth edition. Beirut, 1964.
Sixth edition. Beirut, Mu'assasat Nawfal, [1971].
al-Mağmū'ah al-kāmilah. Vol.3. Beirut, 1971.

Hams al-ǧufūn.
First edition. Beirut, Maktabat Ṣādir, 1943 (?)
Second edition not traced.
Third edition. Beirut, 1959.
Fourth edition. Beirut, 1962.
Fifth edition not traced.
Sixth edition. Beirut, Dār Ṣādir, [1968].
Sixth (!) edition. Beirut, Mu'assasat Nawfal, 1974.
al-Maǧmū'ah al-kāmilah, vol. 4. Beirut, 1971.

Hawāmish.
First edition. Beirut, Dār Ṣādir, Dār Bayrūt, 1965.
Second edition not traced.
Third edition. Beirut, Mu'assasat Nawfal, [1971].
al-Maǧmū'ah al-kāmilah. Vol. 6. Beirut, 1972.

Kān mā kān.
First edition. Beirut, Maṭba'at al-Ittiḥād, 1937.
Second edition. Beirut, Maṭba'at al-Manāhil (Maktabat Ṣādir), 1949.
Third edition not traced.
Fourth edition. Beirut, Dār Ṣādir, Dār Bayrūt, 1956.
Fifth edition. Beirut, Dār Ṣādir, [1960].
Sixth edition. Beirut, Dār Ṣādir, Dār Bayrūt, 1963.
Seventh edition. Beirut, Ṣādir [1966].
Eighth edition. Beirut, Dār Ṣādir, n.d.
Ninth edition. Beirut, Mu'assasat Nawfal, [1971].
Tenth edition. Beirut, Mu'assasat Nawfal, [1974].
al-Maǧmū'ah al-kāmilah. Vol. 2, Beirut, 1970.

Karam 'alā darb.
First edition. Cairo, Dār al-Ma'ārif, 1946.
Second augmented edition. Cairo, Dār al-Ma'ārif, 1956.
Third edition. Beirut, Dār Ṣādir, Dār Bayrūt, 1962.
Fourth edition. Beirut, Dār Ṣādir, Dār Bayrūt, 1964.
Fifth edition not traced.
Sixth edition. Beirut, Mu'assasat Nawfal, (1972).
al-Maǧmū'ah al-kāmilah, vol. 3. Beirut, 1971.

Kitāb Mirdād.
First edition. Beirut, Maṭba'at al-manāhil, [1952].
Second edition. Beirut, 1956.
Third edition, Ṣādir, Beirūt, [1959].
Fourth edition. Beirut, Dār Ṣādir, Dār Bayrūt, 1963.
Fifth edition. Beirut, Dār Ṣādir, Dār Bayrūt, 1966.
al-Maǧmū'ah al-kāmilah, vol. 6, Beirut, 1972.

Liqā'
First edition. Beirut, Maktabat Ṣādir, 1946.
Second edition. Beirut, Maktabat Ṣādir, [1952].
Third edition. Beirut, Ṣādir, 1958.

Fourth edition not traced.
Fifth edition. Beirut, Dār Ṣādir, Dār Bayrūt, 1964.
Sixth edition. Beirut, Dār Ṣādir, [1970].
Seventh edition. Beirut, Mu'assasat Nawfal, [1971].
al-Mağmu'āh al-kāmilah, vol. 3. Beirut, 1970.

Maqālāt mutafarriqah; *al-Mağmū'ah al-kāmilah*, vol. 7. Beirut, 1973.

al-Mağmū'ah al-kāmilah (The Complete Works).
First edition. Beirut, Dār al-'ilm li al-malāyīn.

Vol. 1, 1970.
Sab'ūn vols. I, II, III.

Vol. 2, 1970.
al-yawm al-akhīr; *Liqā'*; *Kān mā kān*; *Akābir*; *Abū Baṭṭah.*

Vol. 3, 1971.
Ğibrān Khalīl Ğibrān; *al-Ghirbāl*; *al-Awthān*; *Karam 'alā darab.*

Vol. 4, 1971.
Hams al-ğufūn; *al-Ābā' wa al-banūn*; *Ayyūb*; *Mudhakkarāt al-Arqash*; *al-Bayādir.*

Vol. 5, 1971.
al-Marāḥil; *Zād al-ma'ād*; *Ṣawt al-'ālam*; *Fī mahabb al-riḥ*;*al-Nūr wa al-dayğūr.*

Vol. 6, 1972.
Durūb; *Ab'ad min Mūskū wa min Wāshinṭun*; *Hawāmish*; *Kitāb Mirdād.*

Vol. 7, 1973.
Yā Ibn Ādām; *Maqālāt mutafarriqah*; *Fī al-ghirbal āl-ğadīd.*

Vol. 8. *Rasā'il*, 1974.

al-Marāḥil.
First edition. Beirut, Maṭba'at Ṣādir, 1933.
Second edition. Beirut, Dār Ṣādir, n.d.
Third edition. Beirut, Dār Ṣādir, Dār Bayrūt, 1961.
Fourth edition. Beirut, Dār Ṣādir, [1966].
Fifth edition. Beirut, Dār Ṣādir, [1968].
Sixth edition. Beirut, Mu'assasat Nawfal, 1971.
al-Mağmū'ah al-kāmilah, Vol. 5. Beirut, 1971.

Mudhakkarāt al-Arqash.
First edition. Beirut, Maktabat Ṣādir, 1949.
Second edition. Beirut, Dār Ṣādir, Dār Bayrūt, 1959.
Third edition. Beirut, Dār Ṣādir, Dār Bayrūt, 1962.
Fourth edition. Beirut, Dār Ṣādir, [1966].
Fifth edition. Beirut, Mu'assasat Nawfal, 1971.
al-Mağmū'ah al-kāmilah, Vol. 4., Beirut, 1971.

Mukhtārāt min Mīkhā'il Nu'aymah.
first edition. Beirut, Maktabat Ṣādir [1948].

Mukhtārāt.
First edition. Beirut, Mu'assasat Nawfal, 1972.

Naǧwā al-ghurūb.
First edition. Beirut, Mu'assasat Nawfal, [1973].

Al-Nūr wa al-dayǧūr.
First edition. Beirut, Dār Ṣādir, [1950].
Second edition. Beirut, Dār Ṣādir,]1958].
Third edition. Beirut, Dār Ṣādir, Dār Bayrūt, 1963.
Fourth edition. Beirut, Dār Ṣādir, Dār Bayrūt, 1966.
Fifth edition. Beirut, Dār Ṣādir, [1969].
Fifth (!) edition. Beirut, Mu'assasat Nawfal, 1973.
al-Maǧmū'ah al-kāmilah, vol. 5, Beirut, 1971.

Rasā'il.
First edition. *al-Maǧmū'ah al-kāmilah.*
Vol. 8. Beirut, 1974.

Sab'ūn. Hikāyat 'Umr. 3 volumes.

Volume 1.
First edition. Beirut, Dār Ṣādir, Dār Bayrūt, 1959.
Second edition. Beirut, Dār Ṣādir, Dār Bayrūt, 1962.
Third edition. Beirut, Dār Ṣādir, [1967].
Fourth edition. Beirut, 1971.

Volume 2.
First edition. Beirut, Dār Ṣādir, Dār Bayrūt, 1960.
Second edition. Beirut, Dār Ṣādir, Dār Bayrūt, 1962
Third edition. Beirut, Dār Ṣādir [1967].
Fourth edition. Beirut, 1971.

Volume 3.
First edition. Beirut, Dār Ṣādir, Dār Bayrūt, 1960.
Second edition. Beirut, Dār Ṣādir, Dār Bayrūt, 1964.
Third edition. Beirut, Dār Ṣādir [1967].
Fourth edition. Beirut, 1971.
al-Maǧmū'ah al-kāmilah, vol. 1. Beirut, 1970.

Ṣawt al-'ālam.
First edition. Cairo, Dār al-Ma'ārif, n.d. The book was advertised as «recently published» in *al-Kitāb*, issue May 1948.

From this first edition three stories were dropped :
'Itāb, Duǧāǧah Umm Ya'qūb, Abū Baṭṭah — they were eventually included in the volume *Abū Baṭṭah.* In the table of contents these three stories were brought together under the heading : *Hawāmish*, which became the title of one of the later collections. The second edition mentions the fact that the three last stories in the first edition have been left out and that they were replaced by three other stories : al-Dīn wa al-dunyā, al-ḥuzn wa al-ḥazānā fuqarā'.

Second edition. Cairo, Dār al-Ma'ārif, [1957].
Third edition. Beirut, Dār Ṣādir, Dar Bayrūt, 1961.
Fourth edition. Beirut, Dār Ṣādir, [1966].
Fifth edition. Beirut, Dār Ṣādir, [1968].
Sixth edition. Beirut, Mu'assasat Nawfal, [1973].
al-Mağmū'ah al-kāmilah, Vol. 5. Beirut, 1971.

Yā Ibn Ādam !
First edition. Beirut, Dār Ṣādir [1969].
Second edition. Beirut, Mu'assasat Nawfal, 1973.
al-Mağmū'ah al-kāmilah, vol. 5. Beirut, 1971.

al-Yawm al-akhīr.
First edition. Beirut, Dār Ṣādir, Dār Bayrūt, 1963.
Second edition. Beirut, Dār Ṣādir [1962].
Third edition not traced.
Fourth edition. Beirut, Mu'assasat Nawfal, 1972.
al-Mağmū'ah al-kāmilah, vol. 2. Beirut, 1970.

Zād al-ma'ād.
First edition. Cairo, Dār al-Muqtaṭaf wa al-Muqaṭṭam, 1936.
Second edition not traced.
Third edition. Beirut, Dār Ṣādir, Dār Bayrūt, 1962.
Fourth edition not traced.
Fifth edition. Beirut, Dār Ṣādir, [1968].
Sixth edition not traced.
Seventh edition. Beirut, Mu'assasat Nawfal, [1972].
One edition was found without date or mention of the edition published by Ṣādir, Beirut.
al-Mağmū'ah al-kāmilah, vol. 5, with the wrong title *Zād al-mī'ād* in the table of contents.

Works of composite authorship, forewords to works of others and translations.

Mağmū'at al-Rābiṭah al-qalamiyyah li sanat 1921. Beirut, Dār Ṣādir, Dār Bayrūt, 1964 (2nd edition).

Ğibrān, Ğibrān Khalīl. *al-Mağmū'ah al-kāmilah li-mu'allafāt Ğibrān Khalīl Ğibrān.* Beirut, Dār Ṣādir, Dār Bayrūt, 1964.

Ayyūb, Rashīd. *al-Ayyūbiyyāt.* Beirut, Dar Ṣādir, Dār Bayrūt, 1959. The same preface has been reprinted in the volumes *Aghānī al-Dārwīsh* and *Hiya al-dunyā* in the same edition.

Works in English.
Original by the author.

The Book of Mirdad.
First edition. Beirut, Sader's Library, 1948.
Other editions. Bombay, 1954.
London, Vincent Stuart, 1962.
New York, Penguin Books, [1971].
London, 1974.

translated by the author.

Gibran Kahlil Gibran.
First edition. New York, The Philosophical Library, 1950.
Other editions, Beirut, Khayats, 1964.
Beirut, Khayats, 1965.

other translations.

The Memoirs of a Vagrant Soul or the Pitted Face. New York, Philosophical Library, 1952.

Till we weet ... (and twelve other stories) Bangalore, 1957.

Mikhail Naimy. A New Year. Stories, autobiography and poems selected and translated by J. T. Perry. Leiden, E. J. Brill, 1974.

Het boek van Mirdad. Haarlem, Rozekruis-pers, 1960.
The same book has been translated into German, Gujarati and Hindi. An English stage-adaptation has been made (Information given by the author).

Translations of poems, essays or stories published in anthologies of modern Arabic literature.

Anthologie de la littérature arabe contemporaine,
Makarius, Raoul et Laura. *Le roman et la nouvelle.* Paris, aux éditions du Seuil, 1964.
Abdel-Malek, Anouar. *Les essais.* Paris, aux éditions du Seuil, 1965.
Norin, Luc et Edouard Tarabay. *La poésie.* Paris, aux éditions du Seuil, 1967.

Kabbani, Sam. *Die Taube der Moschee und andere Syrische und libanesische Erzählungen.* [Stuttgart], Horst Erdmann Verlag, [1966].

Arberry, A. J. *Modern Arabic Poetry.* An Anthology with English Verse Translations. Cambridge, at the University Press, 1967.

Ğibrān's *The Prophet* was translated into Arabic by Nu'aymah.

BIBLIOGRAPHY, GENERAL SECTION

'Abbās, Iḥsān, *Fann al-sīrah*. Beirut, Dar al-Thāqafah, n.d.[2].

'Abbās, Iḥsān and Muḥammad Yūsuf Naǧm, *al-Shi'r al-'arabī fī al-Mahǧar. Amīrkā al-al-shamāliyyah*. Beirut, Dār Ṣādir, [1967][3].

Abdel-Mequid, Abdel-Aziz, *The Modern Arabic Short Story. Its emergence, development and form*. Cairo, al-Maaref Press, n.d.

Abū Māḍī, Ilīyā, *al-Khamā'il*. Beirut, Dār al-'ilm li al-malāyīn, [1965][6].

Amīn, Qāsim Bik, *Taḥrīr al-mar'ah*. [Cairo], al-Maktabah al-sharqiyyah, n.d.[2]

Antonius, George, *The Arab Awakening*. London, Hamish Hamilton, [1955][3].

Al-'Aqqad, 'Abbās Maḥmūd, *Khulāṣat al-yawmiyyah*. republished in *Khulāṣat al-yawmiyyah wa al-shudhūr*. Beirut, Dār al-Kātib al-'Arabī, [1970].

al-'Aqqād, 'Abbās Maḥmūd and Ibrāhīm 'Abd al-Qādir al-Māzinī, *al-Dīwān*. Cairo, al-Sha'b, n.d.[3].

Arberry, Arthur J., *Fifty Poems of Hafiz*. Cambridge, At the University Press, 1947.

——, *Modern Arabic Poetry. An Anthology with English Verse Translations*. Cambridge, At the University Press, 1967.

Arnold, M. *Selected Prose*. edited by P. J. Keating. Harmondsworth, Penguin Books, 1/2 1970.

Beeston, A. F. L. "The Genesis of the *Maqāmāt* Genre", *Journal of Arabic Literature*, vol. II, 1971 p. 1-12.

Blavatsky, H. P. *The Key to Theosophy*. London, The Theosophical Publishing Soc iety, 1893[3].

Bunyan, John, *The Pilgrim's Progress* New York, Airmont.

Cachia, Pierre, *Taha Husayn. His Place in the Egyptian Literary Renaissance*. London, Luzac and Company Ltd, 1956.

Carré, Jean-Marie, *Voyageurs et écrivains français en Egypte*. Vol. I. Du début à la fin de la domination Turque, 1517-1840. Vol. II. De la fin de la domination turque à l'inauguration du Canal de Suez, 1840-1869. Le Caire, Institut français d'archéologie orientale, 1932.

Cheikho, Louis, *Al-ādāb al-'arabiyyah fi al-qarn al-tāsi' 'ashar*. Vol. I. Min al-sannat 1800 ilā 1870. Beirut, al-Maṭba'ah al-kāthūlīkiyyah li al-ābā' al-yasū'iyyīn, 1924[2]. Vol. II. Min al-sannat 1870 ilā 1900. Beirut, al-Maṭba'ah al-kāthūlīkiyyah li al-ābā' al-yasū'iyyīn, 1926[2].

——, *Ta'rīkh al-ādāb al-'arabiyyah fī al-rub' al-awwal min al-qarn al-'ishrīn*. Beirut, Maṭba'at al-ābā' al-yasū'iyyīn, 1926.

Coleridge, Samuel Taylor, *Biographia Literaria*. London and Toronto, J. M. Dent and Sons, New York, E. P. Dutton and Co, [1921] = Everyman's Library no 11.

Cromer, The Earl of, *Modern Egypt*. in two volumes. London, MacMillan and Co, Ltd, 1908[2].

Dāghir, Y. A., *Maṣādir al-dirāṣah al-adabiyyah*. Vol. 1. Sidon, al-Maṭba'ah al-mukhaliṣiyyah, 1961[2]. Vol. 2 : al-Fikr al-'arabī al-hadīth fī siyar a'lāmihi, part 1. al-rāḥilūn (1800-1955). Beirut, al-Ǧam'iyyat ahl al-qalam fī Lubnān, 1955. Vol 3, parts 1 and 2. Beirut, al-Ǧāmi'ah al-Lubnāniyyah, 1972.

Duyvendak, J. J. L., *Lao-Tsu, Tau-te-tsing*. Het boek van de weg en deugd uit het Chinees vertaald en toegelicht. Arnhem, Van Loghum Slaterus' Uitgeversmaatschappij, 1942,

Emerson, Ralph Waldo, *Essays*. 1st and 2nd series. London, J. M. Dent and Co., New York. E. P. Dutton, (1907) = Everyman's Library.

Farag, Nadia, "“The Lewis Affair” and the Fortunes of al-Muqtaṭaf", *Middle Eastern Studies*, Vol. 8, 1 (January, 1972), p. 73-83.

Fénélon, *Les aventures de Télémaque.* (Texte etablie et presenté par Jeanne Lydie Gore). Firenze, Sansoni, 1962.

Freytag, G. W. *Darstellung der arabischen Verskunst. Bonn,* In Commission bei Carl Cnoblauch, 1830.

Ǧabartī, 'Abd al-Raḥmān, *Ta'rīkh 'aǧā'ib al-athār fī al-tarāǧim wa al-akhbār.* new impression. Beirut, Dār al-Fāris, n.d. 3 vols. Translated into French with the title, *Merveilles biographiques et historiques ou Chronique du Cheikh Abd al-Rahman el-Djabarti.* 9 vols. Le Caire, Imprimerie Nationale, 1889-1896.

Ǧabr, Ǧamīl, *Amīn al-Rayḥānī. Al-raǧul - al-adīb.* al-Dawrah, by the author, n.d.

Gabrieli, Francesco, "L'Autobiografia di Mikhail Nu'aima", *Oriente Moderno* XLIX, no. 6-7 (giogno-luglio, 1969), p. 381-387.

Gibb, H. A. R., *Arabic Literature.* Oxford, At the Clarendon Press, 1963[2].

——, "Studies in Contemporary Arabic Literature" I. "The Nineteenth Century", *Bulletin of the School of Oriental Studies* IV (1928), p. 745-760. Republished in *Studies on the Civilization of Islam.* London, Routledge and Kegan Paul Ltd, [1962], p. 245-258.
II. "Manfaluti and the New Style", *BSOS* V (1929), p. 311-322 and *Studies on the Civilization of Islam,* p. 258-268.
III. "Egyptian Modernists". *BSOS* V (1929), p. 445-466 and *Studies on the Civilization of Islam,* p. 268-286.
IV. "The Egyptian Novel". *BSOS* VII, 1 (1933), p. 1-22 and *Studies on the Civilzation of Islam,* p. 286-303.

Ǧibrān, Ǧibrān Khalīl, *al-Aǧniḥah al-mutakassirah* (Broken Wings). Reprinted in *al-Maǧmū-'ah al-kāmilah li-mu'allafāt Ǧibrān al-'arabiyyah.* p. 167-239. Beirut, Dār Ṣādir, Dār Bayrūt, 1964.

——, *'Arā'is al-murūǧ* (Nymphs of the Valley) Reprinted in *al-Maǧmū'ah al-kāmilah ... al-'arabiyyah,* p. 45-81. Beirut, Dār Ṣādir, Dār Bayrūt, 1964.

——, *al-Arwāḥ al-mutamarridah* (Spirits Rebellious) Reprinted in *al-Maǧmū'ah al kāmilah ... al-'arabiyyah,* p. 83-166. Beiert, Dār Ṣādir, Dār Bayrūt, 1964.

——, *The Broken Wings.* New York, The Citadel Press, [1957].

——, *al-Maǧmū'ah al-kāmilah li-mu'allafāt Ǧibrān Khalīl Ǧibrān.* Beirut, Dār Ṣādir, Dār Bayrūt, 1964. Possibly a third edition. Nu'aymah's preface is dated 1949.

——, *Nymphs of the Valley.* New York, Alfred A. Knopf, 1967[10].

——, *The Prophet.* London, William Heinemann, 1956[20].

——, *Spirits Rebellious.* New York, Philosophical Library, 1947. The story "Maḍǧa' al-'arūs" has not been included in this translation of *al-Arwāḥ al-mutamarridah.*

Gogol, Nikolaj W., "De avond voor Sint Jan", *Verzamelde Werken,* Deel I, p. 46-66. Amsterdam, G. A. van Oorschot, 1959.

Hartmann, M. P. W., *The Arabic Press of Egypt.* London, Luzac, 1899.

Hawi, Khalil S., *Kahlil Gibran, His Background, Character and Works.* Beirut, The Arab Institute for Research and Publishing, 1972([2]).

Haykal, Muḥammad Husayn, *Zaynab, Manāẓir wa akhlāq rīfiyyah.* Cairo, Dār al-Ma'ārif, [1974] '.

Heyworth-Dunne, J., *An Introduction to the History of Education in Modern Egypt.* London, Frank Cass and Co., 1968 (reprint).

——, "Rifa'a Badawi Rafi' al-Tahtawi, the Egyptian Revivalist. *Bulletin of the School Oriental Studies,* IX (1937-1939), 961-967, X (1940), 399-415.

——, "Printing and Translation under Muhammad 'Ali of Egypt. The foundation of modern Arabic". *Journal Royal Asiatic Society,* 1940, p. 325-349.

Hilu, Virginia, *Beloved Prophet. The love letters of Kahlil Gibran and Mary Haskell and her private journal.* London, Barrie and Jenkins, 1972.

Hitti, Philip K., *Memoirs of an Arab-Syrian Gentleman or an Arab Knight in the Crusades. Memoirs of Usamah Ibn Munqidh* (Kitāb al-I'tibār). Beirut, Khayats, 1964 — being a republication of *An Arab-Syrian Gentleman and Warrior in the Crusades. Memoirs of Usâmad Ibn Munqidh.* New York, 1929.

Hopwood, Derek, *The Russian Presence in Syria and Palestine, 1843-1914. Church and Politics in the Near East.* Oxford, Clarendon Press, 1969.

Ḥusayn, Ṭāhā, *Al-Ayyām*, vol. 1. Cairo, Dār al-Ma'ārif, n.d. (first edition 1926) vol. 2. Cairo, Dār al-Ma'ārif, n.d. (first edition 1939).

——, *Mudhakkarāt.* Beirut, Dār al-ādāb, [1967]. published also as *al-Ayyām*, vol. 3. Cairo, Dār al-Ma'ārif, [1972].

——, *An Egyptian Childhood.* (= English translation of *al-Ayyām*, vol. 1. London, George Routledge & Sons ltd., 1932.

——, *The Stream of the Days. A Student at the Azhar.* Cairo, Dar al-Ma'aref, 1943. London, Longmans, Green & Co, [1948], revised edition.

Jomard, (E. F.), "Ecole égyptienne de Paris", *Nouveau Journal Asiatique*, Tome II (août 1828), p. 96-117.

Khoury, Mounah A., *Poetry and the Making of Modern Egypt* (1882-1922). Leiden, E. J. Brill, 1971 = Studies in Arabic Literature. Supplements to the Journal of Arabic Literature, Vol. I.

al-Khūrī, Wadī' Rashīd, *Ẓuhūr wa taṭawwur al-adab al-'arabī fī al-mahğar al-amīrkī.* Beirut, Dār al-Rayḥānī, [1963][2].

Lao Tsu, *Tau -te-tsing.* Het boek van de weg en deugd uit het Chinees vertaald en toegelicht door J. J. L. Duyvendak. Arnhem, Van Lohgum Slaterus' Uitgeversmaatschappij N.V., 1942.

Louca, Anouar, *Voyageurs et écrivains égyptiens en France au xixe siècle.* Paris, Didier, 1970.

Mağmū'at al-Rābiṭah al-qalamiyyah li sanat 1921. Beirut, Dār Ṣādir, Dār Bayrūt, 1964 (2nd edition).

Malḥas, Thurayyā, *Mīkhā'il Nu'aymah. Al-adīb al-ṣūfī.* Beirut, Dār Ṣādir, Dār Bayrūt, 1964.

Mandūr, Muḥammad, *Fī al-mīzān al-ğadīd.* Cairo, Maktabat Nahḍat Miṣr wa maṭba'atuhā, n.d. [3].

——, *Muḥādarāt 'an Khalīl Muṭrān.* Cairo, Ma'had al-dirāsāt, al-'arabiyyah al-'āliyyah, 1954.

——, *Muḥādarāt fī al-shi'r al-miṣrī ba'da Shawqī.* Vol. 1. Cairo, Ğāmi'at al-duwal al-'arabiyyah, Ma'had al-dirāsāt al-'arabiyyah al-'āliyyah, 1955.
Vol. 2, idem, 1957. Vol. 3, idem, 1957.

——, *al-Naqd wa al-nuqqād al-mu'aṣirīn*, Cairo, Maktabat Nahḍat Miṣr, n.d.

al-Manfalūṭī, Muṣṭafā Luṭfī, *al-Naẓarāt.* 3 vols. Beirut, Dār al-Thaqāfah, n.d. No reference is made to the first or to other preceding impressions.

Moreh, S., "Poetry in Prose (*al-Shi'r al-Manthūr*) in Modern Arabic Literature", *Middle Eastern Studies*, Vol. 4,4 (July 1968), p. 330-360.

Muğāhid, Zakī Muḥammad, *al-a'lām al-sharqiyyah fī al-mi'ah al-rābi'ah 'asharah al-hiğriyyah min sanat 1301 ilā sanat 1365 (sanat 1883-1936)*, part 4. Cairo, Maṭba'at al-Fağālah al-ğadīdah, 1963.

Mūsā, Salāmah, *Tarbiyat Salāmah Mūsā.* Cairo, Mu'assasat al-Khānğī, 1958.

Musa, Salama, *The Education of Salama Musa.* Translated from the Arabic by L.O. Schuman. Leiden, E. J. Brill, 1961.

al-Muwayliḥi, Muḥammad, *Hadīth 'Īsā Ibn Hishām.* Cairo, al-Dār al-qawmiyyah li al-ṭibā'ah wa al-nashr, 1964.

Nağm, Muḥammad Yūsuf, *al-Qiṣṣah fī al-adab al-ʿArabī al-ḥādith, 1780-1914*. Beirut, Dār al-Thaqāfah, 1966[3].

Naimy, Nadeem, *Mikhail Naimy. An Introduction*. Beirut, American University of Beirut, 1967.

Nantet, J., *Histoire du Liban*. Paris, Les Editions de Minuit, [1963].

al-Nāʿūrī, ʿĪsā, *Adab al-Mahğar*. Cairo, Dār al-Maʿārif, [1967][2].

Nietzsche, F., *Also Sprach Zarathustra*. in *Friedrich Nietzsche Werke in drei Bänden*, Band 2, S. 135-398. Frankfurt, Frankenbuchhandlung, [1971].

Perlmann, M., "The Memoirs of Taha Husayn", *Bibliotheca Orientalis* XXX (1973), p. 13-15.

al-Rayḥānī, Amīn, *al-Rayḥāniyyāt. Wa hiya mağmūʿat maqālāt wa khuṭab wa shiʿr manthūr*. Four parts. Beirut, Yūsuf Ṣādir, 1923. Parts 1 and 2 second edition, parts 3 and 4 first ed.

——, *al-Rayḥāniyyāt*. 2 vols. Beirut, Dār al-Rayḥānī li al-ṭibāʿah wa al-nashr, 1968[7]. This collection should not be confused with the former collection of the same title.

——, *Khāriğ al-ḥarīm*. Beirut, Maṭābīʿ Ṣādir Rayḥānī, [1948][4].

——, *Hutāf al-Awdiyyah*. Beirut, Mu'assasah Dār al-Rayḥānī, 1955.

Rasāʾil Amīn al-Rayḥānī, 1896-1940., ğamaʿahā wa bawwabahā Albirt al-Rayḥānī. Beirut, Dār al-Rayḥānī li al-ṭibāʿah wa al-nashr, [1959].

al-Rayḥānī, Amīn, *al-Muḥālafah al-thulāthiyyah fī al-mamlakah al-ḥayawāniyyah*. Beirut, Dār al-Rayḥānī, 1972. Unknown which edition.

Sakkut, Hamdi, *The Egyptian Novel and its Main Trends, 1913-1952*. Cairo, The American University in Cairo Press, [1971].

Ṣarrūf, Yaʿqūb, *Fatāt Miṣr. Riwāyah fukāhiyyah, iğtimāʿiyyah, tadhhībiyyah*. Cairo, Maṭbaʿat al-Muqtaṭaf, 1922[4].

Ṣāyigh, Tawfiq, "Ğibrān wa Mary Haskell. Qiṣṣat ʿalāqah", *Hiwār*, 22, May-June, 1966, p. 5-48.

——, "Aḍwāʾ ʿalā Ğibrān. Ḥayātuhu al-thaqāfiyyah " *Hiwār* 23, July-August, 1966, p. 5-43.

al-Sayyid, Shafīʿ, *Mīkhāʾīl Nuʿaymah. Manhağuhu fī al-naqd wa ittiğāhuhu fī al-adab*. [Cairo], ʿĀlam al-Kutub, 1972.

al-Sharīf, Ḥasan, "Nahḍat al-adab fī Miṣr", *al-Hilāl*, vol. 27, (1918), p. 67ff.

al-Shidyāq, Fāris, *Kitāb al-sāq ʿalā al-sāq fī mā huwa al-fāryāq, aw ayyām wa shuhūr wa aʿwām fī ʿağam al-ʿArab wa al-aʿğām*. Cairo, Yūsuf Tūmā al-Bustānī, Maktabat al-ʿArab, n.d.

Shukrī, ʿAbd al-Raḥmān, *Dīwān*. Ğamaʿahu, wa haqqaqahu wa qadamahu Niqūla Yūsuf. Alexandria, al-Maʿārif, 1960.

Ṭarrāzi, al-Fīkūnt Fīlīb dī, *Taʾrīkh al-ṣiḥāfah al-ʿArabiyyah*. Beirut, al-Maṭbaʿah al-adabiyyah, 1913.

Taymūr, Maḥmūd, *al-Shaykh Ğumʿah wa aqāṣīṣ ukhrā*. Cairo, al-Maṭbaʿah al-salafiyyah wa maktabatuha, 1927.

Tibawi, A. L., "The American Missionaries in Beirut and Butrus al-Bustani", *Middle Eastern Affairs*, Number 3 (St. Anthony's Papers, Number 16), p. 137-182. London, Chatto and Windus, 1963.

Tibawi, A. L., *American Interests in Syria, 1800-1901, A Study of Educational, Literary and Religious Work*. Oxford, Clarendon Press, 1966.

Ṭūsūn, Prince ʿUmar, *al-Baʿathāt al-ʿilmiyyah fī ʿahd Muḥammad ʿAlī, thumma fī ʿahday ʿAbbās al-awwal wa Saʿīd*. Alexandria, Salāḥ al-Dīn, 1934.

Wild, S., "Friedrich Nietzsche and Gibran Kahlil Gibran", *al-Abḥāth* 22, nrs 3 and 4 (December, 1969), p. 47-57.

Wordsworth, William, "Preface to Lyrical Ballads 1800, 1802" in *Penguin Critical Antholo-*

gies : *William Wordsworth*, edited by Graham McMaster, p. 38-64. Harmondsworth, Penguin Books Ltd, [1972].

al-Yāziǧī, Nāṣīf, *Maǧma'at al-Baḥrayn*. Beirut, Dār Ṣādir, Dār Bayrūt, 1961 (reimpression).

Young, Barbara, *This Man from Lebanon. A Study of Kahlil Gibran*. New York, Alfred A. Knopf, 1967.[14].

Zakkā, Ṭunsī, *Bayna Nu'aymah wa Ǧibrān*. Beirut, Maktabat al-Ma'ārif, 1971.

Zaydān, Ǧurǧi, *Ta'rīkh ādāb al-lughah al-'Arabiyyah*, part 4 new impression redone and commented upon by dr Shawqī Dayf. Cairo, Dār al-Hilāl, n.d.

al-Zubaidi, A. M. K., "The Dīwān School", *Journal of Arabic Literature*, vol. I, p. 36-48.

TITLE INDEX OF WORKS BY MĪKHĀ’ĪL NU‘AYMAH

References are to pages.
Italicized references are to the footnotes on the indicated pages.

INDEX OF POEMS BY MĪKHĀ'ĪL NU'AYMAH

References are to pages.
Italicized references are to the footnotes on the indicated pages. References in bold type indicate that a poem or a fragment of one is cited in transcription followed by a translation.

GENERAL INDEX